KV-371-713

Contents

Contents

Other Easy Step-by-Step Guides by Pauline Rowson include:

Telemarketing, Cold Calling and Appointment Making

Marketing

Building a Positive Media Profile

Being Positive and Staying Positive

Successful Selling

Communicating with More Confidence

Fundraising for Your School

Marine Mysteries by Pauline Rowson published by Fathom:

Tide of Death

In Cold Daylight

All the above are available from any good bookshop or direct from:

Rowmark Limited
enquiries@rowmark.co.uk
www.rowmark.co.uk

Easy Step by Step Guide

Publishing and Promoting Your Book

Pauline Rowson

Rowmark

Published by Rowmark Limited
65 Rogers Mead
Hayling Island
Hampshire
PO11 0PL

ISBN 0 9548045 3 8

Note: The material contained in this book is set out in good faith for general guidance and no liability can be accepted for loss or expense incurred as a result of relying in particular circumstances on statements made in this book.

Edited and typeset by
Frances Hackeson Freelance Publishing Services, Brinscall, Lancs
Printed in Great Britain by RPM Reprographics Ltd. Chichester.

Contents

Contents

About the author

Pauline completed her first adventure novel aged eight and has been writing ever since both for pleasure and profit. She ran her own marketing and publicity agency for over ten years before becoming involved full time in publishing and writing.

In 1998 she set up her own publishing company and has since published seven of her own titles and twelve by other authors, all branded as Easy Step by Step Guides. These books are currently sold in the UK, South East Asia, South Africa, India and Russia.

Pauline is also author of *Tide of Death*, an Andy Horton Marine Mystery, and *In Cold Daylight*, a marine mystery/suspense novel.

As well as a writer and publisher Pauline is a popular conference speaker. She gives author talks and conducts workshops on writing and self-publishing. She has lived in Wiltshire and Northern Ireland, before returning to her native Hampshire.

Introduction

Why do we write?

We write because we enjoy it, because we have something to say, because we want to immerse ourselves in another time and place, because we wish to create, inform, educate or entertain, because it is a hobby that very often turns into an obsession. We do not write to become rich and famous (although that would be nice!) and many of us know that the financial rewards in pursuing a writing career are not great.

For all of us who write there is no greater reward, or sense of satisfaction, than seeing our work in print. Getting into print, though, is extremely difficult. This book sets out to make that task easier. It also looks at how, having got into print, you can maximize sales of your work.

Why are you reading this book?

There could be many reasons why you are reading this book:

1 your book is so specialist that it is difficult to place with a publisher, or you are having difficulty finding a publisher

2 you wish to retain control of your work: the design, sales and marketing and therefore wish to self-publish

3 you have a publisher but need to maximize sales and promote your book.

The aim of this book

Whatever your reasons for writing and for reading this book I hope it will help you to understand:

- how the publishing industry works
- how you can successfully self-publish your work
- how you can market and sell your work.

At the very least it will provide food for thought.

How to use this guide

This guide is written in a clear step by step style to help you to gain the best understanding possible. I recommend that you read it through from beginning to end and then dip into it to refresh your memory. The boxes in each chapter contain tips to help you and at the end of each chapter is a handy summary of the points covered.

1
The publishing climate

The climate for publishers today is extremely difficult and fiercely competitive. Profit margins are being squeezed by the increasing cost of producing books and by the ever higher discounts demanded by some of the larger booksellers and the supermarket chains. The days when a publisher used to take a risk on an unknown author and let him or her build sales over a few titles are gone – or almost gone. Now, to get your work published you have to go **big** right from the word **go**, or you have to have a name that can generate sales pre-publication.

In response to a tightening market, many publishers are seeking economies of scale. This means they are merging to form bigger publishing houses, creating even fewer opportunities for new writers to get their work published.

But it's not all bad news

- there are now many smaller independent publishers who are producing a wide range of interesting books and selling them

- there are many independent booksellers who are seeking interesting and varied books for their customers

- books are being sold in specialist retail outlets, for example Past Times, which stocks nostalgia books and biographies; outdoor equipment shops, which carry a range of walking books; chandlers sell sailing books; garden centres a variety of books including children's and general interest; some newsagents carry books and main Post Office branches are soon to introduce selling books

- books are also sold by direct mail and the Internet

- new technology has enabled books to be produced digitally allowing short print runs, thereby opening up the market to the self-publisher and small publisher

- the popularity of e books is increasing and the growth in the media has opened up many more opportunities for the self-publisher and small publisher to promote their books.

As you can see there are now many opportunities for you to both publish and promote your book.

So where do you begin?

Know your market

> You have an idea for your book, or your book is already written; first consider what type of book it is.

Publishing is about categories and some books simply do not fit into a category. That doesn't mean to say that they won't sell, they can and do but it can be more difficult because you are unable to pinpoint exactly what type of person, or group of people, will buy your book.

> The more you know about your target customers (readers) the more successful you will be. This is because you will be able to find them and communicate with them more effectively.

Fiction

If you write fiction then try and identify what kind of fiction. Visit a local bookshop and see the categories on offer. For example:

- crime
- romance
- historical
- literary

- fantasy
- sci-fi
- erotic
- adventure
- thriller
- contemporary
- chick lit
- children's fiction
- teenage fiction

And that's just to name a few.

Non-fiction

Again, there is a wide range. For example:

Specialist subjects:

- travel
- hobbies
- military history
- health
- biography

Sector specific:

- education
- business
- academic

And, of course, there are many other categories including poetry, anthologies, short stories ...

> So try categorizing your book. Can you sum up in one phrase what type of book it is?

For example, I write crime novels, thrillers and suspense stories, which are marketed as 'Marine Mysteries' – they all have a theme or setting that is based in and around the sea.

The Easy Step by Step Guides are business, management and self-help books.

Identify your reader

The more clearly you can define your book the easier it is to identify your readers.

For example:

- are your readers mainly male, female or of both sexes?

- What would their typical age range be?

- Where do they come from? Where do they live?

- Where do they shop?

- What kind of social and economic background are they from?

- What is their lifestyle?

- How do they spend their leisure time?

- What type of work are they engaged in, or are they retired?

- Which newspapers and magazines do they read?

- Is your book aimed at a particular ethnic group?

- If it is a children's book then what is the target age range of the reader?

Whether you've written fiction or non-fiction do you have a clear picture of the type of people who would buy your book?

> You need to get to know who your potential readers are because then you can find them and target them.

The majority of customers of Easy Step by Step Guides are business customers, but business covers a wide range. Are the readers directors of multinational companies or are they more likely to be the self-employed person? It is no good me sending a mailshot to senior executives if my kind of books do not appeal to them.

Rowmark's management and marketing books are generally bought by small business owner/managers, students and self-employed people.

Rowmark's self-help/personal development books are not only bought by the above but also by individuals, mainly women between the ages of thirty and sixty.

The Easy Step by Step Guide to Fundraising for Your School is bought by those involved in education.

This book is bought by people like you – writers.

Once you have a clear idea of who is most likely to buy your book, you can then find out where they are and decide how to approach them i.e. how to promote your book to them.

My crime novels, for example, are targeted at people who like reading crime so I approach crime reading groups, writing conferences dedicated to crime or that have a crime-writing session on the agenda, crime magazines, crime book web sites, crime specialist bookshops etc.

Because they are also *Marine Mysteries* I can target other groups, for example the sailing community and associated companies like the ferry operators, chandleries and marinas etc.

As I live in Hampshire I can target my local geographical area, for example Portsmouth and the surrounding areas, the South Coast, the Isle of Wight.

But what if I think **everybody** will be interested in my book?

Then think again, they won't. Besides how can you promote your book to everybody? It would cost a fortune. Running advertising poster campaigns on train stations and the Underground, and taking advertising space in the national newspapers and magazines would run into hundreds of thousands of pounds.

> You need to target your efforts and make your money and your marketing work.

In addition, if you were to target **'everybody'** what message do you use? It would have to be one that would appeal to a very wide range of people with diverse interests and backgrounds. This means that sometimes your marketing message will hit the right note with the right people, the rest of the time it will be wasted and so will your money.

> Don't waste time and money chasing readers who are unlikely to buy your book.

For example it would be foolish of me to spend money on targeting teenagers or the children's fiction market.

Once having decided **where** your book sits and **who** to target, you can then decide **how** to target them. Where can you advertise, for example? What other promotional tools would they respond to? More about this in later chapters but if you don't undertake this first basic exercise of identifying just what type of book it really is and whom it might appeal to, then you could be promoting your book to the wrong people – a waste of time and money.

Once you have decided who will buy and read your book ask yourself some further questions:

- How large is that group of customers? – Will I be able to sell a lot of books or is it a limited audience?

- Where are they and how easy is it for me to reach them?

- How many books are there already in the marketplace like mine?

- How is my book different to all the others on this subject? What is its unique selling point?

- How much is it going to cost me to reach my readers?

In summary

- publishers are operating in a climate that is not conducive to publishing those works that carry a high risk

- major booksellers and the supermarket chains are squeezing profit margins by demanding higher discounts on titles

- the advent of digital print and the Internet has created opportunities for smaller publishers and those wishing to self-publish

- know your market – what type of book are you writing or have written?

- the more you know about your target customers (readers), the more successful you will be in reaching them and communicating with them

- How will your book be different to all the others on this subject in the marketplace? What is its unique selling point?

2
Finding a publisher

If you choose to go down the route of trying to find a publisher for your book you must first ensure that you do your research. What type of publisher takes your type of book? It is no good wasting your time, and the publisher's, by submitting work that they are not publishing, for example sending fiction to a non-fiction publisher. You can do your research in a number of ways.

- look through the *Writers' and Artists' Yearbook* and make a note of the publishers you'd like to try, or refer to *Cassells Directory of Publishing*.

- identify books in your local bookshop or library that are in the same category as yours, and make a note of the publisher. Then search for that publisher in the above named directories or on the Internet

- check if they will take submissions; they may even provide guidelines on how to submit your work to them

- attend writers' conferences where you are able to

meet with publishers and literary agents. There are many of these worldwide. Find out what is happening in your district or area, ask at your local arts centre, or library, or search the Internet

- subscribe to the trade press – *Publishing News* and *The Bookseller* in the UK give you news and information on publishers, the market, new works commissioned, contacts, information on bestsellers plus much more.

- attend book fairs in your country. The London and Frankfurt Book Fairs are particularly lively and packed with publishers from all over the world. There are now many other book fairs taking place around the world. Browse around the stands, pick up catalogues from publishers and see what type of work they publish. Don't try and sell your work to them at these fairs: the big book fairs are primarily for selling rights for contracted books to overseas publishers, for increasing exports of books and for creating awareness and boosting sales of books to booksellers. You are unlikely to meet the commissioning editors here and even if you do they will have little or no time to talk to you.

- Attend writing courses where you can improve your craft and meet guest lecturers, authors, literary agents and publishers.

Finding a literary agent

Do you need an agent and if so how do you find one?

Some of the larger publishing houses no longer take submissions direct from authors but only through an agent and finding an agent is as difficult as finding a publisher. Even when you do find an agent there is no guarantee that he or she will be able to find you a publisher. This is extremely frustrating for the author and disappointing for both author and agent. Although they have contacts in the publishing houses, agents are operating in the same publishing climate as you.

Making submissions

Your chances of getting published can be ruined by a poor submission. Publishing houses receive hundreds if not thousands of submissions a year so make sure that your submission is professional.

Fiction submissions

Your work should be typed using double spacing and wide margins in Times New Roman 12 point type. It should be typed on one side of white A4 paper only. Do not use fancy coloured paper as it will make the typescript hard to read and will only annoy the editor. Do not staple pages together or bind them in any way, they will only have to be unbound and many editors (or submissions departments) will not even bother to do this. Put a large elastic band around the bundle and a hard piece of cardboard to support it through the mail. Post in a Jiffy bag or similar; only email if they say submissions will be accepted by email. Send a covering letter and enclose return postage if you want a reply and your manuscript returned to you. Always keep a copy of the manuscript and wordprocessing files, and first check that these are exactly the same version as that submitted to the publisher.

Always comply with the publisher's or agent's request when submitting your work; if they say they want only two chapters then send them two chapters not four. Also always send the first two chapters and not two chapters picked out at random. If they say they want a two-page outline then send only this.

Make sure the copy you send is clean and tidy without coffee stains, torn or dog-eared. If it has done the rounds it may look the worse for wear so print off a fresh copy. With wordprocessing facilities there is no excuse for it looking tatty.

Be professional. Keep a record of your submissions and only chase by a polite telephone call, email or letter after six weeks. You can try multiple submissions, sending your work out to more than one publisher/agent at a time.

Put the title of your book at the top of each page in the left hand corner along with your name, for example:

Tide of Death/Rowson

And the page number on the top right hand corner.

Tide of Death/Rowson   1

Keep trying

If your submissions don't succeed keep trying. Try not to be too disappointed, although I know how incredibly difficult this is. If someone takes the time to give you some constructive feedback welcome it and take a fresh look at your work. Can you improve it? Are you approaching it from the right angle?

> **Keep writing and keep improving.**

The non-fiction outline

This should include the following:

- an outline of what the book covers, chapter by chapter
- chapter headings
- state if the book will have illustrations/ photographs and if so what kind and who will be drawing/taking them. Perhaps include a few samples of the illustrations if these are already prepared. Picture quality, the source and cost are crucial for many non-fiction books.
- the target market for the book
- the market generally for this type of book and why you think yours is different – what is its unique selling point
- your credentials for writing this book – a brief CV
- the first chapter or possibly the first two chapters.

Again, put the title of your book and your name on the top left-hand corner of the manuscript and the page number on the top right-hand corner.

The covering letter

Address the letter to the publishing or commissioning editor or agent asking if they would consider the enclosed manuscript. Once again, adopt a professional approach, use white A4 paper only, type or wordprocess the letter. Only hand-write the letter if your writing is legible. Include in your letter:

- the type of book it is – the category
- the target reader
- any details of previously published work
- any details of competitions you have won
- a brief résumé and any other interesting points about yourself.

Literary consultancies

> A literary consultancy is not the same as a literary agency.

A literary consultancy can offer you an unbiased critique of your work. This can be very helpful. The standard of literary consultancies vary, some provide excellent value for money giving feedback line by line, others do little more than provide you with a brief letter of critique.

The Hilary Johnson Authors' Advisory Service offers professional appraisals of typescripts for both unpublished and published authors including novels, full-length non-fiction, short stories, children's books, poetry, radio/TV/film scripts, etc. They also have specialist readers available for science fiction/fantasy, crime, Harlequin Mills & Boon, etc. In addition, there is a copy-editing/proofreading service, which could prove valuable if you decide to go down the self-published route.

Beware the literary consultant who flatters or offers unrealistic expectations. A frank assessment is not always comfortable, but anything less than this is unlikely to be helpful.

You can choose a literary consultancy from among those who advertise regularly in reputable writing magazines, like *The Author,* (The Society of Authors magazine) or *Writing Magazine,* or those who are listed in yearbooks, such as the *Writers' and Artists' Yearbook.* Be suitably cautious when dealing with anyone advertising on the Internet only.

In summary

- do your research – what type of publisher/literary agent takes your type of book?
- don't waste time and money sending your manuscript to the wrong people
- ensure your submission is as professional as possible
- do comply with the publisher's/agent's request when submitting your work
- always send the first two chapters and not two chapters picked out at random
- send your submission with a brief covering letter and enclose return postage if you want your manuscript returned
- keep a record of your submissions and only chase

by a polite telephone call, email or letter after six weeks

- if you don't succeed keep trying, keep writing and keep improving.

3
Self-publishing

Self-publishing is not a last resort, it may in fact be a first resort. As I mentioned before it is now a viable option for many writers. But what exactly does it mean and how does it differ from vanity publishing?

Self-publishing means that you organize the editing, typesetting, printing and production of your book, overseeing the whole project and ending up with the finished product. The books are yours to do with as you please at the end of the day.

> You become the publisher and remain in control of the whole process.

Vanity publishing

Vanity publishing is where you pay a sum of money to a company who will produce the book for you. Check carefully the credentials of these companies. Many claim that they will market your book for you and in fact don't. Others ask you for money to conduct advertising campaigns for your book, which never materialize. If you send your manuscript to a vanity publisher you may get a glowing report from them, on the back of which they ask to be allowed to publish the book but for a fee. Always be wary of this. You could find yourself handing over large sums of money for little in return.

Hopefully by reading this book you will have a greater knowledge of just what is involved in publishing and promoting your book and therefore the questions you should ask any vanity publisher before committing to anything.

Self-publishing your book

So let's look at how you set about achieving this. Before the book is ready to be printed you need to get it from the manuscript stage into its final form. This usually first involves a copy-editing process.

Copy-editing

If you do not know who to choose to edit and proofread your work then consult The Society for Editors and Proofreaders who produce an annual directory. The electronic edition of the directory is available on the Internet in searchable format at www.sfep.org.uk. From this list you can pick out those who live locally to you, or who have expertise in your subject or category. Get an estimate of costs and ask if they can provide you with testimonials.

An editor

An editor will edit your book, knocking it into shape for you, correcting your punctuation if necessary, examining sentence structure and the overuse of certain words or terms (we all have them) and suggesting alternatives. He or she will suggest where you might re-write, some may even re-write for you, if you wish.

Some editors prefer to edit on-screen, others prefer to work with your hardcopy but you should still supply your wordprocessing files, as they may wish to use the disk to search for key words. Most copy-editors now prefer email as the means of corresponding with you. Generally a copy-editor will send you a list of 'author queries' once they have completed the editing. These are points to be resolved before the editing can be completed and may relate to your writing style, particular spellings or inconsistencies etc.

Always ask the copy-editor how much they charge. They may price their work by the manuscript page or on an hourly rate but you need an estimate for the complete project.

How long will they take to edit? What is their workload and when will they be able to schedule in your book?

Typesetting

Publishers employ in-house or freelance designers to design the book ready for the typesetter, indicating the page layout, margins, typeface/s, typesizes, illustration positioning and sizes. A freelance book designer can be costly and difficult to find, so you may like to ask your copy-editor for advice on the layout, alternatively many typesetters will prepare a sample page layout for you. You can show the typesetter books you like the appearance of so they can base their layout on these.

Occasionally you may find a person who can act both as typesetter and editor. Again check on timescale and charges.

As with all relationships, personal chemistry is important so ensure you find someone who understands what you are trying to achieve and who you can work with.

Look for advertisements in professional magazines, ask others for their recommendations, ask your printer if they can recommend anyone.

A few editors and typesetters will guide you through the self-publishing process and have a great deal of experience in this market, but generally they specialise in their own particular area.

Book size

When deciding on the size of your book take advice from the printer but also look for books that are similar to yours and compare sizes. Does your book need to be A format – the standard paperback size – or B format, the larger size? Is it a large hardback illustrated book or a children's book? There are all sorts of book sizes and most have a technical name, or at least a name given to that size in the industry. Don't worry too much about this, just take a sample with you to the typesetter or printer or measure the book you are comparing yours with and give the dimensions to the printer.

> Do not agree on a special or new size.

This will not only cost you a fortune to print but will meet with resistance from the bookseller stocking your title as it might not fit neatly on their shelf space. It may also cost you more in envelopes if you are sending books out direct to fulfil customers' orders or to bookshops; you could end up having to buy a larger size of envelope or worse having special ones printed.

For a glossary of book trade terminology see a very useful web site www.osi.hu/cpd/resources/paglossary.htm#pa

Finding a printer

There are now many specialist book printers who will help guide you through the self-publishing process. Many can also help you with designing the bookjacket or cover and the interior book layout and can advise on typesetting, paper, format, obtaining an ISBN (International Standard Book Numbering) and ensure that the bookjacket carries a bar code. If they can't help directly then they can usually put you in touch with others who can help you.

Some printers also provide distribution services fulfilling your book orders, or they work with others to provide this. What most printers (if not all of them) do *not* do is market and sell your book for you. That is down to you.

> Printers will print your book, they are not publishers – you are the publisher.

Not all printers will have an understanding of, or experience in, book printing. A simple telephone call to them followed by a visit (if possible) will help you check them out. Ask to see samples of their work. If they can't show you books that they have previously printed then don't use them unless you are one hundred per cent confident they will do a good job for you.

How do they print?

There are two types of printing processes: lithographic and digital.

Digital printing

Digital printing uses the latest in computer technology to produce short print runs very cost effectively. This means you can test the market before committing yourself to larger print runs and incurring high costs. Or you may simply wish to have a small number printed to give to your friends and family. Digital printing allows you to print just one book, fifty, one hundred or more, and usually up to five hundred copies before the printer switches to the more traditional form of printing called lithographic or litho printing.

Digital printing is capable of producing high quality colour photographs. It can also produce jackets and covers although these are generally produced using the more traditional lithographic printing (see below).

With digital printing the unit cost is usually higher than if you were to have your book printed by the more traditional method of lithographic (litho) printing which can run into quantities of thousands to hundreds of thousands, but there is no point in printing thousands and only selling about one hundred. It will tie up your capital (cost you more) and you will have storage problems – where are you going to keep all those books?

Lithographic printing

Whilst digital printing will suit most people's requirements, lithographic printing can be an option if your book is mass market fiction. There are a number of printers who specialize in this area and the best way to track them down is to examine the inside pages of books that are similar to your own, where the name of the printer is given, and contact that printer for an estimate of costs. Generally the lowest quantity they would print would be about two thousand copies and for smaller quantities they would not be prepared to quote as they could not be cost-effective.

Costs vary from printer to printer so it is advisable to get two or three quotes for comparison purposes before making a decision.

It is easy to be over-optimistic about how many books you think you will sell and go for large quantities when in fact it might be better financially to produce a smaller number. One way that Rowmark manage smaller print runs of their business books is to print the covers for the books using lithographic printing in quantities of five hundred. The printer then stores these for us and we can print off one hundred or so books when we require them.

Printing costs vary not only between printers but also between countries and it is now common practice for many publishing houses to print outside the UK. By all means consider an overseas printer, which may be considerably cheaper than a UK printer but you will need to manage carefully the quality, timing and delivery issues that this brings with it.

Questions to ask a printer

Before agreeing to proceed ask the printer:

- what type of printing equipment do they have, – i.e. can they print digitally and therefore produce short print runs of your book. What is the minimum short run they can print for you – one book? Twenty books? Five hundred books?

- What experience do they have of the book printing market? Can they show you samples of books they have previously printed?

- Do they have in-house designers or illustrators, or connections with designers and illustrators who they can recommend? Can you see some examples of their work? How much extra might this cost?

- Do they have connections with copy-editors and typesetters or can they assist you with this?

- Do they provide any other services once the book has been produced? For example, they might have a web site and offer to put your book on their web site with a link to your own web site.

- What sort of timescales do they work to? How quickly can they turn around your book?

- What sort of options are there on binding your book – should it be hardback or paperback, and can they do either?

- What are their charges? How much will it cost you for different print runs?

- How do they like to receive the work? Many printers prefer to receive a pdf file and will charge extra to convert from Word format. If your book is hand-written then you will need to build in the cost of getting someone to key it onto disk for you.

- Can they help you with obtaining an ISBN and can they insert a bar code on your jacket cover?

Printers can be found through advertisements in magazines like *Writing Magazine* and at writers' conferences, or through personal recommendation. You can contact the British Printing Industries Federation (BPIF) and ask their advice. Alternatively look at the title page of published books that are similar to yours and see who printed it. Look them up on the Internet or contact the BPIF for details and then ask them to quote.

Before we leave the subject of printers it might be worth mentioning here e-books. You may decide not to print your book at all but go straight to producing an e-book – considerably cheaper as there are no associated printing costs. Or you may decide to produce an e-book as well as a traditional printed book.

e-books come in a number of different formats and you will probably require the services of a specialist to make your material compatible. This will obviously cost you. There are e-publishers who will help you with this and showcase your book on their web sites and possibly others for a fee. This is a new and growing market so tread cautiously here before parting with any money, check submission statements and terms and conditions of contracts before making any commitment.

Type of paper

There are so many different papers that it can be extremely confusing for the lay person, and sometimes for the printer. Look at the type of book you are publishing and compare it to others, what kind of paper do they use? What does it look like, is it cream or white? What is its weight – is it thick or fairly thin and limp? Smooth or rough? Does your book need to accommodate illustrations and photographs which need a good quality, smooth white paper?

Before speaking to the printer try and get clear in your mind how you would like the finished product to look and feel. I did not want the Easy Step by Step Guides printed on cheap, cream and fairly rough paper that I refer to rather unflatteringly as toilet paper. I wanted a nice crisp, clean feel and look – slightly more expensive but image was important.

Choose a paper that is suitable for your market and your book. In addition, choose a printer's stock paper and not one that has to be specially ordered, as it will substantially increase your costs and cause problems when reprinting.

> Ask to see paper samples both loose-leaf and bound into a sample book that will give you some idea of the quality and feel of the finished product.

Binding

The printing industry has its own jargon when talking about binding which may confuse you – it certainly confuses me e.g. limp, sewn, perfect bound etc. Essentially you need to decide how you want your book to appear, is it a hardback or a paperback? Is it stapled or sewn into the binding? You do not necessarily have to produce a hardback copy of your book but can go straight into paperback if you wish; again this depends on the type of book you are publishing.

Ask the printer to show you samples of different bindings and explain them to you. Look at other books that are similar to yours and see how they are bound; do you wish to emulate that? Is it the norm?

(Jackets, covers and price are discussed in chapters 4 and 5.)

Do I need an ISBN and what is it?

In order for your book to be found by a potential buyer you will need to apply for an ISBN. This is not complicated.

If you do not have an ISBN then your book cannot easily be sold through the bookshops.

In order to get an ISBN you need to apply to the ISBN Agency who will send you an application form to complete and some notes on how to complete it. ISBNs are sold in a block of ten so you will need to purchase this amount even though you may have no intention of using any more than one. Any publisher is eligible to apply for an ISBN providing they have a qualifying product available for general sale or distribution to the public.

When you apply for an ISBN you will need to give the name of your publishing company. This does not mean that you have to form a limited company but simply come up with a name.

You will need to enclose with your application page samples of your title page and title page verso.

Example title page

Publishing and Promoting your Book

Pauline Rowson

Example title page verso

Published by:
Rowmark Limited
65 Rogers Mead
Hayling Island
Hampshire PO11 0PL
Copyright © Pauline Rowson 2006

It takes ten working days for you to receive your ISBN so allow this in your schedule although there is a fast-track service offering a three working day period but you will pay extra for this.

By registering for an ISBN you are ensuring that your title is available on a database that can be accessed by the bookseller, distributor and librarians. This information is also used by many of the online booksellers and you will find that your book appears on online sites without you having to do anything. For further details on this contact ISBN Agency (address supplied at the back of this book).

In summary

- self-publishing means that you organize the editing, typesetting, printing and production of your book, overseeing the whole project and ending up with the finished product
- vanity publishing is where you pay to have your book published
- there are now many specialist printers who will help guide you through the self-publishing process
- some printers can assist with bookjackets and covers, typesetting and editing, and applying for an ISBN (International Standard Book Numbering)
- ask to see samples of books the printer has already produced
- check if the printer can print digitally enabling you to have a short print run, and get estimates of costs
- when deciding on what size your book should be look for those books that are similar to yours and compare sizes
- choose a paper that is suitable for your market and your book
- ask the printer to show you samples of different

books to see how they are bound

- in order for your book to be found by a potential buyer you will need to apply for an ISBN.

4
Pricing

Normally prices are set depending on a number of factors. For example:

- your market – UK, overseas
- your type of book – fiction, non-fiction, children's, illustrated
- your competitors – what they currently charge for a similar type of book
- the cost of producing the book

Whilst the above is still relevant we now also need to take into account new entrants into the book market – the Internet and the supermarkets – and the discounts they demand, which has put downward pressure on book prices.

Most publishing houses have now switched from calculating mark-up to gaining volume sales in the hope of achieving profit. Volume sales for the self-publisher may not be possible. Of course you may sell a considerable number of your books but probably not thousands or hundreds of thousands, though I'd be very happy to be proved wrong. So how do you set your price?

Setting your price

First study the market. How much do other books similar to yours cost? Do you wish to be on a par with these or are you going to make your book cheaper with the hope of encouraging readers to purchase it? Beware though the psychology of pricing; will readers perceive that your book isn't as good as the competitors because it is cheaper and therefore choose the competitor's book rather than yours?

You may wish to add up all the costs of producing your book, add on a little profit and charge the customer that price. A word of caution here though – beware of pricing yourself out of the market. If your book ends up retailing at £20.99 when everyone else's is £6.99 I don't think you will have much success in selling it. In addition, by setting a high price you may give out the message to the bookseller that you don't expect to sell many!

When looking at how you set your prices you need to consider the following:

- your objectives – do you wish to make a profit or simply cover your costs? Are you prepared to make a loss? How much profit do you wish to make and over what period?

- your costs for producing the product (book) and delivering it to the market:
printing costs
typesetting and editorial

jacket design
ISBN cost
admin and postage costs

- the competition
- the demand for your book
- distribution channel mark-up (see chapter 7)
- the discounts you are offering (see chapter 7)
- your marketing costs (see chapter 8)

Budgeting

Before proceeding with your self-publishing venture you should work out a budget so that you know more or less what your costs will be.

To do this you need to get estimates of costs for:

- editing
- typesetting
- printing –after deciding what your print run will be (allowing in this a quantity of free copies, which you will need to give away for book reviews and to others)
- design and artwork of the jacket or cover
- purchase or commissioning of any photographs or illustrations
- marketing – see following chapters
- delivery and other sundry costs like petrol costs to deliver your books to the bookshops or wholesalers
- postage and packaging

- telephone costs for chasing up payment of invoices
- your time, if it is distracting you from your main form of earning.

Also consider how long will it take you to sell all your books? Does it matter to you? Does your book have a certain shelf life?

You may wish to revisit this chapter after having read through the rest of this book when you might have a clearer idea of your potential spending on marketing.

In summary

- normally prices are set depending on a number of factors:
  your market
  your type of book
  your competitors
  the cost of producing the book

- when looking at how you set your prices you need to consider:

- your objectives
  your costs for producing the books and delivering them to the market
  the competition
  the demand for your book?
  distribution channel mark-ups
  discounts
  overheads
  marketing costs

- before proceeding with self-publishing you should work out a budget

---

5

Making your book stand out

There are thousands of books printed every year and many do not even sell two hundred copies, so how do you make your book stand out?

Here are some things that you need to think about:

- branding
- image – especially the bookjacket or cover
- uniqueness – what makes your book different?
- quality of writing

Why brand?

What matters is not merely that people know about your book but how they feel about it. People tend to buy what they are familiar with, which is why when we find an author we like we avidly buy the rest of his or her books. If the author changes his style we can sometimes become disappointed and if they produce a book that is not their best it may prevent us from buying their next book. There is a saying in writing and publishing circles – 'You're only as good as your last book'!

Branding the style of book, or books, could help your reader to make a choice. For example all our Easy Step by Step Guides are branded as such and have the same style no matter what the title so this helps people to know what they are buying. They know they are getting books simply written, with lots of bullet points, tips and minimal jargon. Books that provide them with straightforward practical advice, and all our authors need to be aware of this and write in this style.

My crime fiction is branded as *'Marine Mysteries'*.

You can also compare your books with others to place them. For example my Easy Step by Step Guides are often compared to my competitors Kogan Page. My thrillers/suspense are in the style of Robert Goddard and my detective novels are akin to Reginald Hill and Robert Barnard rather than the hard-boiled crime that is associated with Ian Rankin.

All this helps to place your book in the market and therefore make it easier for people to find it and buy it.

Branding is used to define identity and helps people relate to the product.

Building a brand

Various factors go into making up a brand. These

include:

- the book itself – its style and the quality of writing
- the packaging – the jacket/cover, the size of the book, the quality of the paper
- the advertising – where it is being placed, what kind of advertising, the images used, and the style of copy writing
- the brand name – the imprint, logo and we can extend this in the book buying business to perhaps the names of the characters
- the author – what type of books he or she is known for
- the price – as discussed in chapter 4.
- how and where the book is sold and distributed – as discussed in chapter 7.

And finally, what reinforces the brand is the consistency of all the above.

Choosing a brand name for your publishing venture

If you need to choose a name for your publishing business or imprint, which you will invariably have to in order to obtain an ISBN, then think long and hard about what name to choose. It can be a very tricky area and marketing history is littered with expensive errors. Essentially the brand name should:

- never contradict the essential product qualities i.e. the qualities of the book
- not have unfortunate connotations

- be easy to say, pronounce, catchy
- fit onto the spine (or at least the logo or an abbreviation of the name will have to)

But who is the brand – the publisher or the author?

An interesting question.

If I gave you a publisher's name and then asked you to sum up what your image or impression of that publisher is, and the type of books they publish, would you be able to? Possibly not. But If I asked you to sum up the author and what he or she stands for then perhaps you can. Ian Rankin – hard-boiled crime; Erica James – contemporary, romantic; Clive Cussler – adventure.

As an author can you build a brand for your books?

Bookjackets

The bookjacket is a very vital part of marketing and promoting your book and one that can be very difficult to get right. Take expert advice, listen to it and also view the competition; what do the covers look like on their books? Can you emulate it? Or do you want to pioneer something?

I know fashions come and go but your cover is the first thing that could attract a potential buyer.

Think about it: you call into a bookshop and browse the shelves in the category of book you desire; what makes you pick up a certain book?

It may be the author – you know his or her reputation, you have read or heard about him, you like his style or you are curious to read him.

Or if you don't know the author you scan the spines or look at the cover – does it look interesting, tempting, inviting, is it your sort of book?

You then turn the book over and read the blurb on the back. Sound interesting?

You go to the first page and you read the first few lines – are you hooked? Do you like that style of writing? Yes. The price is good, you make the purchase.

So here, as you can see, a number of factors have come into play, which we have been discussing namely:

- the author's reputation or brand/style of writing
- the jacket image
- the copywriting skills on the back of the book
- the quality and style of writing on the first page
- the price

If all these factors are right the purchase is made and if the reader enjoys the book he will search out more by the same author. If getting hold of these proves difficult then we have a problem. You want your readers to be able to buy your book easily so how it is distributed and where it is sold is important (more about this in chapter 7).

Let's return to the jacket or cover. Make it the best you possibly can. Study the market and the competition and engage the services of a good designer. Brief them on the book's subject and its market, giving them details of the book's emphasis or a summary of the contents. Provide information on the author for background. Decide if your bookjacket is to be produced in one-colour, two-colour or four-colour (full colour) printing. When I first started the Easy Step by Step Guides I produced one colour only book jackets as money was tight and I was still testing the market. This may be applicable to you but as mentioned before it really does depend on the type of book and the market. Four-colour will obviously cost more so you will need to budget for this but it may be possible to get away with two-colour; ask your designer and printer for advice, but also have a clear idea in your own mind as to what might be suitable to avoid being pressurized into adopting a more expensive option when it is not really necessary.

Write a good blurb or get someone who is expert in this to write it for you, a marketing or sales person perhaps.

Supply the 'copy' or wording for the jacket or cover to the designer as a word-processing file and clearly state what you want on the front, the spine, the back and the jacket flaps, if applicable. Be careful with spelling and grammar and proofread the jacket or cover proof very thoroughly.

Your bookjacket is a vital promotional tool and ideally should be available at least four months in advance of publication so that you can use it to send out to booksellers. You can drop the image of the front cover onto an Advanced Title Information Sheet, which is used to promote the book to the trade. (See chapter 6)

Reviews

If you can get review quotes on the back of the jacket, or even on the front, then so much the better, although research has shown these have less impact than a good jacket design and blurb.

In order to get reviews you will need to send your book to reviewers in advance of publication.

Publishers may do this by sending out proofs bound with the finished jacket/cover but you may not be able to afford printing covers in advance. A colour computer-generated printout of the design can suffice, with photocopied proofs of the book. You can then gather any reviews, select brief quotes and include these in the final jacket/cover design.

I have obtained reviews for my own books by simply sending out the manuscript and asking my contacts to review it and provide me with a quote. I have only sent manuscripts though to people and magazine reviewers I know or have checked with first to ensure they are happy to receive it in this format.

In summary

- make your book stand out from others through:
  branding
  image – jacket/cover
  uniqueness
  quality of writing

- branding the style of your book or books could help your reader to choose your book

- write a good blurb or get someone who is expert in this to write it for you

- your bookjacket should be available in advance of publication so that you can use it to send out to booksellers and others

6

The publishing cycle

When I first started working in the publishing industry it took me a long time to get the hang of the publishing cycle and I think this is true for many authors. I had been used to the fast industry of marketing and media where everything had to be done immediately. But producing a book and getting organized for marketing it and then selling it takes time. So I think it would be helpful here if I gave you an outline of how the publishing industry works and how you can pick up a few tips from it and emulate some of the practices yourself to boost success.

Advanced Title Information Sheets

Once a book is commissioned an Advanced Title Information Sheet will be drawn up by the publisher, commonly referred to as an AI. This becomes your first selling tool. This is sent to reps, wholesalers and bookshops. I draw up an AI sheet for each new title usually six to nine months in advance of publication and email or send it to my reps working overseas, my UK rep and to my rights manager who are then able to sell to their contacts in the wholesale, retail and publishing sectors.

The AI sheet contains the following information:

- the title of the book
- the author's name
- the size of the book in mm
- information on the title
- classification
- the ISBN
- number of pages
- binding
- publication date
- price
- and any other relevant information for example, marketing angle for the book, target market, its unique selling points, location or special setting, sales of the author's last book if appropriate.
- any noteworthy points about the author

Example AI Sheet

See pp. 48–49 for an example AI.

This Advanced Title Information Sheet will be shown along with jacket proofs to the key buyers from the book chains and to wholesalers.

You may not employ reps and rights agents yourself but can produce an Advanced Title Information Sheet

Fathom

|ADVANCED TITLE INFORMATION|

A NEW MARINE MYSTERY INTRODUCING DI ANDY HORTON

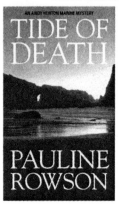

It is DI Andy Horton's second day back in Portsmouth CID after being suspended for eight months. Whilst out running in the early morning he trips over the naked battered body of a man on the beach. PC Evans has been stabbed the night before, the DCI is up before a promotion board and Sergeant Cantelli is having trouble with his fifteen-year-old daughter. But Horton's mind is on other things not least of which is trying to prove his innocence after being accused of raping Lucy Richardson.

Beset by personal problems and aided by Cantelli, Horton sets out to find a killer who will stop at nothing to cover his tracks. As he gets closer to the truth, and his personal investigations start to uncover dark secrets that someone would rather not have exposed, he risks not only his career but also his life...

Publication date: 29 March 2006
Classification: Contemporary Crime/Mystery
ISBN: 0 9550982 0 3
Author: Rowson Pauline
Price: £6.99
Format: A format (178mm x 111mm)
Number of pages: 432pp
Binding: Paperback

About the author
Pauline Rowson is author of seven business and self help books. This is her first crime novel. She is a professional conference speaker and for ten years ran her own Marketing and PR Agency. She lives on Hayling Island, Hampshire, England.

Marketing Campaign
Nationwide author talks to writing groups, libraries, writing conferences. National press and magazine reviews. Postcards and Posters. Mailing Campaigns. Point of Sale material. Regional Advertising Campaign. Tie-in with marinas and yacht companies. Southampton and London Boat Show author signings.

Trade Orders and Distribution
Gardners Books Limited. 1 Whittle Drive, Eastbourne, East Sussex Tel: 01323 521777 Fax: 01323 525504 www.gardners.com

A Marine Mystery - published by Fathom (an Imprint of Rowmark Ltd.)
Rowmark Limited 65 Rogers Mead, Hayling Island, Hants. England PO11 0PL
Telephone: + 44 (0) 23 9246 1931, Fax: + 44 (0) 23 9246 0574 e mail: enquiries@rowmark.co.uk
www.rowmark.co.uk

Fathoming out another Marine Mystery!

ADVANCE TITLE INFORMATION

EASY STEP BY STEP GUIDE TO
PUBLISHING AND PROMOTING YOUR BOOK

Publishers are taking fewer risks when it comes to publishing unknown authors, so finding a publisher for your work can be extremely difficult. Your book may be so specialist that it is difficult to place, or you may wish to retain control over the design of your own work, its sales and marketing and therefore self publish. Whether published or self published you will certainly need to market and promote your book in order to stimulate sales. This book will show you:

* how the publishing industry works
* how to submit your work to publishers and agents
* how to successfully self publish your work
* how to sell your book in the UK and overseas
* how to market your book
* how to publicise your book

Author: Pauline Rowson
ISBN: 0 9548045 3 8
Price: £9.99
Size: 216mmx135mm
Binding: Paperback
Number of Pages: 128
Published: February 2006

About the author
Pauline Rowson is a successful author and publisher. She started as a self publisher and now runs a fully fledged independent publishing company. Her background is in Marketing and PR and she is author of several sales, marketing and motivational books. She is also a popular conference speaker on a variety of subjects.

Classification
Self help/writing

Easy Step by Step Guides are:
* Quick and easy to read - from cover to cover in two hours
* Contain a handy bullet point summary at the end of each chapter
* Provide lots of tips
* Have a simple style and layout – making the books easy to read
* Jargon free – straightforward and easy to understand
* Strong branding – making it easy for readers to find and collect the titles
* Written by practitioners - people with real experience and who are 'experts' in their subject

Advertising and marketing
Author promotion at talks, seminars and workshops
Direct mailing campaigns, Magazine and journal reviews

Publisher: Rowmark Limited 65 Rogers Mead, Hayling Island, Hampshire. England PO11 0PL Tel: + 44 (0) 23 9246 1931 Fax: + 44 (0) 23 9246 0574 e mail: enquiries@rowmark.co.uk www.rowmark.co.uk

for your own book and send it to all your local bookshops and other retail outlets that might be interested in stocking your book. You can then follow it up with a telephone call or visit them.

If you wish to sell further afield then you can buy mailing address labels from the Booksellers Association who also produce a directory called *The Booksellers Directory* (see chapter 7).

Catalogues

Most publishers produce an annual catalogue. This is used as a selling tool to send to bookshops, send direct to readers in some cases, and for display and distributing at the London Book Fair, the Frankfurt Book Fair plus other book fairs that the publisher may attend.

Many publishers also take advertising space in the marketing material produced by the wholesalers.

You can produce your own marketing material, a flyer, poster or postcard and whilst exhibiting at international book fairs may be beyond you, or of no interest to you, you can still use this material to target your reader and booksellers – more on this in later chapters.

Most of the marketing is done just before or around the release of the title, (a book launch is another marketing activity which I discuss in chapter 14) but it is important to try and keep the momentum going after publication which is where a media profile can help you. Again this is discussed in chapters 9,10,11 and 12.

For now let's return to the publishing cycle.

Bibliographers

Once you have your ISBN and have prepared your Advanced Title Information Sheet you can register your book with all the relevant bibliographers.

Nielson BookData

You can considerably enhance your title entry with Nielson BookData by adding content to the basic information you have completed and supplied when you registered for your ISBN. For example you can add a jacket image, a description of the book, biography of the author, the book's table of contents etc. but in order to do so you will need to subscribe to this service and for one title you may not think it worthwhile. Contact Nielsen BookData for further information or visit their web site at www.nielsenbookdata.com

Bowker

Bowker, the US ISBN Agency, actively entered the UK market in 2005. For more information on registering your book with them visit their web site at www.bowker.co.uk.

Bibliographic Data Services Limited (BDS)

BDS provides a bridge between the publisher and library. They specialize in the provision of information to libraries and library booksellers. You can register for free. Tel: 01387 702251 or email: info@bibdsl.co.uk

> Bibliographic information goes to booksellers, librarians and others around the world. It is important therefore to ensure that your book has an ISBN and is listed with as much information as possible, otherwise it has little chance of being found and therefore being purchased, or loaned, by the reader.

After publication

Legal deposit

Once published you have a legal obligation to deposit your material in designated libraries or archives. The six legal deposit libraries are:

The British Library

The Bodleian Library Oxford

The University Library Cambridge

The National Library of Scotland, Edinburgh

The Library of Trinity College Dublin

The National Library of Wales, Aberystwyth

Publishers are required to deposit with the British Library within one month of publication. The other libraries have a right to claim publications from publishers and distributors.

For depositing with the British Library you should send your copy to:
The Legal Deposit Office
The British Library
Boston Spa

Wetherby
West Yorkshire LS23 7BY

The other five legal deposit libraries employ an agent to collect on their behalf. Copies should be sent to:

Copyright Libraries Agency
100 Euston Street
London NW1 2HQ

For further information on this, and a leaflet entitled 'Legal Deposit', email legal-deposit-books@bl.uk or visit www.bl.uk or telephone 01937 546268.

Registration for Public Lending Rights (PLR)

If your book is purchased by a library then you may be eligible for payments under the PLR scheme. Authors and illustrators living in the EEC plus Liechtenstein, Norway and Iceland, can qualify. Registration is free and an application form can be obtained from www.plr.uk.com.

Payments are made once a year in February and are proportionate to the number of times (established from a sample of libraries) that your book has been lent out from Public Libraries.

Authors' Licensing and Collecting Society (ALCS)

The ALCS's main business is to collect and distribute money from sources where writers cannot act as individuals. These include:

- photocopying licensing schemes
- German Public Lending Rights for British Authors
- retransmission of British films, TV and radio programmes on European cable networks.

You can register journals, articles and books with the ALCS who will collect any money due to you and issue payments once a year. For further information contact 020 7395 0600 or email alcs@alcs.co.uk www.alcs.co.uk

Publishers Licensing Collecting Society (PLCS)

This acts in the same way as the ALCS but for the publisher. So if you are both author and publisher why not also register with this organization? Telephone: 020 7299 7730 or email pls@pls.org.uk www.pls.org.uk

In summary

- once a book is commissioned an Advanced Title Information Sheet is drawn up commonly referred to as the AI
- it is important that your book is listed with all the relevant bibliographers
- once published you have a legal obligation to deposit your material in the six legal deposit libraries
- you may be eligible for payments under the Public Lending Rights scheme, the Authors' Licensing and Collecting Society, the Publishers Licensing Collecting Society (PLCS).

7

Selling the book

Having published your book you need to tell people about it, otherwise how can they purchase it? This can be a complicated and expensive process depending on how many copies of the book you'd like to sell, the type of market for your book and its potential readership. But even the most surprising of books can become best-sellers, with it hardly costing anything, by word of mouth recommendation.

Before we look at how to promote our book, let's first explore how books are sold. There are many different levels involved in the bookselling industry:

- the distributor
- the wholesaler
- the bookseller/library/retailer/others
- the customer/reader

So you can sell your books in a number of ways:

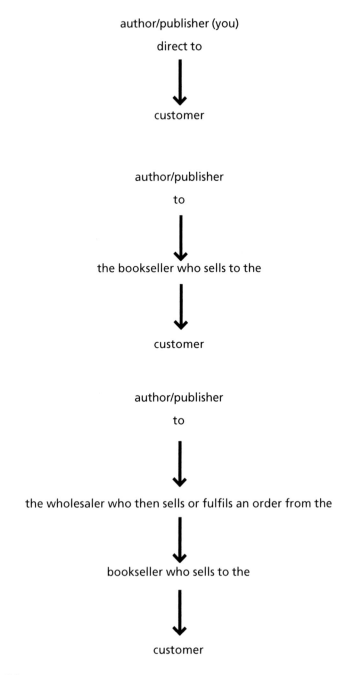

author/publisher (you)

direct to

↓

customer

author/publisher

to

↓

the bookseller who sells to the

↓

customer

author/publisher

to

↓

the wholesaler who then sells or fulfils an order from the

↓

bookseller who sells to the

↓

customer

Getting all these channels to work in tandem takes a great deal of effort and sometimes a lot of luck not to say money. For example you may be very good at promoting your book to the customer via talks, and local and national media coverage, as a result of which the customer goes into a bookshop to buy your book only to find the bookshop doesn't sell it. The bookseller then has to order it from your distributor/ wholesaler who doesn't hold stocks of it, or who has run out of copies, so they then have to order it from the publisher. By the time a copy reaches the bookshop you just hope the customer is still keen on buying it.

So let's forget about the customer for the moment and return to him later. Let's also take the author – you – out of the equation for the time being and look at the trade end of bookselling.

Who sells books?

- the bookseller
- the wholesaler or distributor

Selling to booksellers

There are specialist reps and agencies that sell into bookshops and these can range from a substantial organization to a one-man band. If you wish someone to do your selling for you then you will have to pay for this. Some reps work on a commission-only basis others will charge a monthly fee. If you only have one book then you could find it rather an expensive exercise and you might be better off identifying and targeting booksellers yourself and contacting them through sending marketing literature and/or following up with telephone calls. You can of course call at your local booksellers in person with literature supporting your book and a copy of the book and ask if they would stock it.

If you find a rep or agency and approach them they may well turn you down. This is because the book may not be suitable for their list (the other publishers they represent) or they feel they cannot justify representing one title.

Booksellers can comprise of a number of different organizations for example:

Bookshops

The traditional booksellers are both independent bookshops and the large bookshop chains.

Online booksellers

There are now many online booksellers, the biggest and the most well known of which is Amazon.

Supermarkets

Now in addition to buying your toilet rolls in the supermarket you can pick up a copy of the latest bestseller.

Specialist retailers

Some specialist retailers carry books in their high street stores and sell them by mail order and on their web sites. For example if your book is about sailing then a chandlery might wish to stock it and promote it not only in their shop but also through their mail order catalogue and on their web site. If your book is about gardening then a garden centre or nursery may wish to stock it and again promote it through their customer mailing list.

Associations and institutes

Then there are specialist organizations, associations and institutes who also have their own online bookshops; sometimes they have retail bookshops or they may sell books at conferences or through member mailing lists, newsletters and magazines.

Discounts to booksellers

Whoever sells your book will want a discount – and why not – they have to make a living too. So allow for this and offer them a reasonable discount. Normally the discount to a retailer is around 35 per cent of the retail price of your book but some will ask for considerably more than this, some less. Some specialist organizations may ask for 50 per cent discount and the big supermarkets and the large bookselling chains can often ask for anything up to 80 per cent. This means that even if you were able to get your book into that outlet you would probably be doing so at a loss, or making very little money. This might be acceptable to you in return for the chance of seeing your book in one of the major outlets, or your objective might be to take a loss on certain outlets, sacrificing profit for increased exposure.

When fulfilling a book order yourself direct to a bookseller, you may wish to charge postage and packaging on single orders.

Of course it is disappointing when a bookseller does not wish to stock your book but there are thousands of books published every year (2,500 a week according to Nielsen BookScan 2005) and with only a certain amount of space in the shops in which to sell them it is not surprising that so many don't get stocked. In addition, new titles are being produced all the time and it is not possible for shops to stock books that they do not have a call for.

Targeting booksellers

You will probably already know your local booksellers, possibly having bought something from them in the past. You can call on them, introduce yourself and show them your book (or your Advanced Title Information Sheet and bookjacket if you are trying to drum up interest for orders in advance). Ask them if they would like to stock them or do some kind of promotion. Their response will be dictated by the size and type of the bookshop and your type of book. If they do not wish to take your book don't be offended; they may need a little persuading or it may be because it really is not their market.

If they do take a few copies, or usually just one, they will most likely want it on a sale or return basis, i.e. if it doesn't sell within a period (could be three weeks but ask them) then it will be returned to you. Or they will telephone you and ask you to collect it. In order to make your book 'sell through' you need to promote it. I examine how you can do this in the following chapters.

You may wish to produce a small poster. Ask the bookshop if they can display it, or print small postcards or bookmarks to have on the counter to give away. The same can be done for your local libraries.

But what if you want to sell your book to bookshops in a wider geographical area?

As mentioned before you can obtain a directory from the Booksellers Association, which lists bookshops in the UK and Ireland. The directory is arranged geographically by town and contains full name and address details. The head offices of the large bookselling chains are also provided. Under each entry are details on the stock range held so you can trawl through this directory and identify all those bookshops that carry your type of book and target them with a flyer and possibly a follow-up telephone call.

Alternatively the Booksellers Association can conduct a search of their database for you identifying the bookshops that carry your type of book and you can purchase mailing labels from them, or the data in electronic form.

One word of caution here, booksellers receive a great deal of literature so make sure that your promotional leaflet or your Advanced Title Information Sheet is both eye catching and informative.

Amazon

Amazon has been a boon for both the reader and the self-publisher. It offers an opportunity for you to sell your book online. If you have obtained an ISBN your book will automatically be listed on Amazon. To enhance that listing and to increase sales you can register under the Amazon advantage programme, which allows you to add further information about your book. Obviously Amazon has the right to refuse to take books that they feel unsuitable, for example if it were offensive or obscene. Amazon requires a discount, which is usually between 50 per cent and 60 per cent of the retail price. Visit their web site to check out the details on www.amazon.co.uk/advantage for more information and to register.

Once you have registered and have been accepted, orders for your book will be e-mailed to you and you will need to log on using your chosen password to pick up your orders. As all transactions are conducted electronically you will need to be able to access the Internet to sell your book via this method, unless your orders are fulfilled through a wholesaler.

Selling overseas

This can be difficult if you only have one book. Generally speaking you would need to find an overseas agency or representative who can sell on your behalf and many, if not all, will be reluctant to take you on with only one or a handful of books.

You can of course target overseas libraries and booksellers direct but this would be costly and a lengthy operation in identifying them, targeting them and then following them up.

You could join the Independent Publishers Guild (IPG) and take space on their stands at international book fairs like Frankfurt and London. You don't necessarily have to attend the fair yourself but the staff of the IPG will take messages from anyone interested in your title. Or you could attend in person and try and arrange some appointments direct with overseas buyers by looking through the catalogues produced at these fairs and writing to those you identify as possible targets. In addition, if your title is on display at the book fair it might attract the attention of an overseas buyer.

Alternatively you could band together with other self-publishers to form a co-operative organization and try and sell your books in this way having strength in a higher number of titles.

The Publishers Association and UK Trade and Investment have produced a very helpful publication covering export sales, called *Guide to export for UK Publishers*. Whilst not all the contents may be applicable to you it certainly makes interesting reading and can provide valuable information on overseas sales, mailing, distribution and shipping. Contact details are provided at the back of this book.

Selling to wholesalers/distributors

Where does a wholesaler or distributor fit in and do you really need one?

The answer may very well be no, especially if you have only one book (unless it is a very big and fast seller in which case you may be so inundated with orders that you cannot handle it).

Distributors will distribute your book to the buyer who could be the customer direct or more usually the bookshop, retail outlet or online bookshop. Distributors warehouse stocks of books and process returns from the bookshops (unsold copies). Some can and do perform other tasks for publishers including telesales and publicity and some also have their own sales team, but in the main they are a warehouse, distribution and fulfilment centre. A list of distributors can be found in *Cassell Directory of Publishing*.

Wholesalers take a stock of your book/s and then distribute them to the bookseller when that bookseller places an order for your book. Again some wholesalers have a sales team but essentially they provide an order fulfillment service. Both distributors and wholesalers produce marketing material and target bookshops, libraries and other outlets to stimulate sales.

Discounts to distributors/wholesalers

Distributors and wholesalers will want a fee for their services which is usually a discount against the retail price of the book. This can vary from 30 per cent to 55 per cent.

With one title it can be difficult to secure a distributor or wholesaler and of course you may not need one, depending on how many books you print and the level of your sales.

The following chapters cover how you can sell and promote your book direct to the customer.

In summary

- Booksellers can comprise of:
  bookshops
  online book sellers
  supermarkets
  specialist retailers

associations and institutes

- whoever sells your book will want a discount
- call on your local booksellers, introduce yourself and show them your book (or your Advanced Title Information sheet and bookjacket if you are trying to drum up interest for orders in advance)
- if they do take a few copies, or even just one, they will most likely want it on a sale or return basis

---

8

Promoting your book

So let's now look at how you can promote your book.

What promotional tools can you use?

This will depend on possibly two factors:

- how much money you have to spend i.e. your budget
- how much time you can devote to promoting the book

We'll start with what is most probably the most expensive form of promotion – advertising.

Advertising

Not only is it the most expensive but it can also be the most ineffective, especially if you haven't got a **big** budget to spend on it. Advertising is usually beyond the means of the self-publisher and indeed even the small independent publishers. National advertising in newspapers, magazines and on television and radio costs thousands of pounds so unless you have won the Lottery, or are very wealthy and don't mind parting with your money, I would advise against it, with the exception of small-scale advertising possibly in local or specialist publications. If you do decide to advertise then make sure the publication you are advertising in will reach your target reader i.e. the sort of people who would be most likely to buy and read your book. Research the media and then either visit the publication's web site or telephone them to obtain details of their readership and circulation. This information is usually contained in what is called a media pack, which also includes a copy of the latest publication.

You may wish to advertise in the trade press, for example *Publishing News* or *The Bookseller* to make bookshops and others in the trade aware of your forthcoming title. Or your wholesaler may produce a magazine or buyers guide. If so, ask about costs and then judge whether this would be a good investment.

Poster advertising could be worthwhile but for the self-publisher and small independent publisher this is most likely to be posters that can be given out to bookshops, local libraries, Church halls etc. rather than poster campaigns on hoardings, railway platforms, bus shelters, buses and the Underground, which would be very expensive.

When advertising make sure that your advertising copy works for you.

- Does the jacket image stand out?
- Have you got a good caption to grab the attention?

- Is the copy strong enough to attract potential buyers of your book?

- Is it memorable?

The golden rule of advertising is that it must conform to AIDA:

A   **A**ttention – grab the attention

I   **I**nterest – build interest

D   **D**esire – stimulate desire

A   **A**ction – prompt action

For more on how to make your advertising work see *The Easy Step by Step Guide to Writing Advertising Copy.*

Promotional items

Can you produce any giveaways that can be given out when you do your talks? Or perhaps you can leave them in the local library, bookshops and other places of interest? These can be in the form of postcards, bookmarks, pens, carrier bags, etc. When printing your jackets or covers ask the printer if you can use any surplus white space around the printed area to reproduce a postcard or a book mark, which will show the front cover of your book. This could also provide some brief information on the book including the ISBN, the price, number of pages and a contact address or telephone number for enquiries. This is a very cost effective way of obtaining additional promotional literature and can cost little more than printing the jackets or covers alone.

Direct marketing

Building a database of your readers and target readers and mailing them with details of your book can be a very effective way of marketing. You can also build an email list and email your contacts when your new book has been launched or is about to be launched. As an independent publisher with many titles we produce a catalogue and regularly mail this to people who have bought books direct from us. We also buy other mailing lists of business people and mail them. For The Easy Step by Step Guide to Fundraising for Your School we mailed schools and local education authorities. For this publishing guide we mailed writing course providers, writing workshops, conferences, literary consultancies and others.

Your database should contain at least:

* what your reader has bought from you
* how the reader heard of you
* their name and address plus other contact details

Editorial

This is one of the most cost-effective ways of promoting your book and because it should play such a key part in your promotion I have devoted chapters 9, 10, 11 and 12 to it.

Writing articles

You can offer to write articles for your target media in exchange for some publicity around your book. (For more on this see chapter 13 plus our sister publication *The Easy Step by Step Guide to Writing Newsletters and Articles.*)

Taking a stand at exhibitions and trade fairs

These don't have to be big exhibitions and trade fairs but perhaps those that are relevant to the subject matter of your book, or that are local to your area. For example, if your book is about crafts then a local craft fair might be a good place to exhibit your book and give out some of those bookmarks, display that poster, sign copies and sell books.

As an independent publisher we are members of the Independent Publishers Guild and because of this we are able to exhibit our titles at the London Book Fair and at the Frankfurt Book Fair at reasonable costs.

When deciding to exhibit you will need to ask what it will cost and take into the account the following:

- cost of the space
- cost of hiring or producing a stand
- cost of material
- cost of your time
- cost of travelling

Talks

Talk, talk, talk, about your book to anyone and everyone who will listen. This can be very painful for some authors who would much rather sit in their study or back bedroom and write. There are now so many writing groups and reading groups all of whom would probably love to hear from you. In addition, there are women's groups, business groups, special interest groups and so on. Research them all and write to them, sending a promotional flyer about your book and your details, asking them if they would like you to speak. Some organizations may even pay you to do this but don't expect it. If they don't then consider carefully before refusing; it could be a good opportunity for you to publicize your book and sell a few copies. (For more on this see chapter 13)

Sponsorship

Maybe you can team up with a company or organization that will help to promote your book. Perhaps you can donate a share of your royalties or profits to a charity and in return they will promote your book on their web site and in their newsletter or magazine.

Word of mouth

Books with very limited marketing have still managed to achieve huge success. Much of this has been derived through word of mouth. If people like your book they'll recommend it to others.

Allow in your budget for a number of free books to give away to key people who could be very influential in recommending it on to others.

Use your contacts

Keep your address book up to date and trawl through it for any contacts who might be helpful.

Send copies with a short personal note to anyone influential.

Send details of your book to all your relatives and friends at Christmas with their Christmas card.

Web site

Ensure that you have a web site. It doesn't have to be grand, simply provide interesting and entertaining information about you and your book/s. Your web site can also include information on where and how to order and any details about forthcoming books. If you are published rather than self-published, it can also provide a link to your publisher's web site.

In summary

- advertising is probably the most expensive form of promotion

- produce posters that can be given out to bookshops, local libraries, church halls etc.

- when advertising make sure that your advertising copy works for you.

- the golden rule of advertising is that it must conform to **AIDA**

- produce giveaways that can be given out when you do your talks
- build a database of your readers and potential readers and mail them with details of your book
- build an email list and then email your contacts when your new book has been launched or is about to be launched.
- editorial is one of the most cost-effective and effective ways of promoting your book
- attend trade fairs which are relevant to the subject matter of your book, or which are local to your area.
- tell people about your book, telephone your local bookshops and visit them in person
- give talks to groups
- team up with a company or organization that will help to promote your book.
- donate a share of your royalties or profits to a charity for help in promoting your book
- send copies of your book with a short personal note to anyone influential
- send details of your book to all your relatives and friends at Christmas with their Christmas card
- ensure that you have a web site.

9

Promoting your book – getting publicity

Getting national reviews of your book may be difficult but don't despair because there are lots of other opportunities to get your book into the media spotlight.

Dealing with the media can be an awesome experience; some people would rather go to the dentist than handle the media.

Some have difficulty in understanding what makes a good news story; others do not have the time to write news releases and liaise with the media; and some are afraid that the media will twist everything they say.

All these problems can be overcome. But why bother in the first place? Publicity is a powerful tool – it carries at least two and a half times the weight of advertising and it is an extremely cost- effective way of promoting your book. And the best way of getting media coverage is to send in what is called a 'news release'.

The days when journalists were truly roving, looking to pick up a good story are long gone. They have to rely on information coming to them; they are very busy people often working to extremely tight deadlines, so if you can help by writing the story for them so much the better and the greater your chance of getting into print.

But the news release has to be written in a certain way in order to boost your chances of gaining media coverage. This is covered in the following chapter; first you need to understand how the media work.

The difference between editorial and advertising

Advertising is **bought** space so within reason you can say what you like in that space.

This means that *you* have control over what you say.

Editorial coverage is **not** bought space. It is therefore best to assume that you have no control over what is said.

This can be difficult for some people to grasp. Yes, journalists do sometimes get names and figures wrong and occasionally misinterpret what you have said either by accident or, dare I say it, by design – but there are ways of writing your news release that will minimize any errors or misinterpretations by the journalist (this is explained in chapter 10).

You also have no guarantee that, having sweated over your story for hours and sent it to the newspaper or magazine, it will appear. Telephoning the journalist and sounding off is not a good idea. It will only alienate him or her. If your story doesn't get used there could be several reasons for this:

- it has been squeezed out by something else
- you got the timing wrong and missed the deadline
- you failed to explain the significance of your book to the journalist
- your news release was badly written and too long
- it was due to plain editorial incompetence!

Perseverance is the key. If your news release doesn't get used can you think up another one, or another angle? If possible try and keep a regular steady flow of news stories going to the journalist.

Understanding editorial style

Most people know the difference in style between a tabloid newspaper and a broadsheet, i.e. the difference between the *Sun* and the *Daily Telegraph.* These newspapers write for different audiences and therefore the content and style of their newspaper will reflect this.

> Editorial style is something you need to bear in mind when submitting your news release to different types of media.

A weekly newspaper may have a very different style and editorial content to that of a daily newspaper.

Trade and specialist magazines will carry a more technical or detailed story than local newspapers.

So you will need to tailor your release to suit the media you are targeting. Working on computers with cut and paste facilities make this task relatively easy.

Getting on to television and radio

Getting on to television and radio is more difficult than getting into print, simply because television and radio do not have the same amount of 'space' dedicated to news stories. By all means research the radio or television station and the most suitable programmes for your news story and submit your news release to the producer of that programme, or to a correspondent or reporter, but bear in mind that radio and television get many of their news stories from the press. So even though you may not have targeted radio or television with your news release you may still nevertheless find yourself being interviewed. I talk more about being interviewed in chapters 11 and 12.

Using a publicist

If you don't fancy writing your news releases and handling the media yourself then you may wish to engage a publicist. If so you will obviously have to budget for this. Most publicists charge by the hour, which can be anything from £30 per hour to £150 per hour! But some may give you a cost for handling a one-off project, for example your book launch. Try and find a publicist who has some experience of book publishing. The Publishers Publicity Circle web site could be a good place to start: www. publisherspublicitycircle.co.uk

Understanding the media

Editors and journalists have a job to do and that job is to produce newspapers or magazines that their readers want to buy, or to fill broadcast programmes that people want to listen to and watch. Try to provide them with stories they will want and which are suitable for their medium.

Always try and be accessible

The media work to extremely tight deadlines so if a journalist telephones you for a comment or for further information then ensure you are available to take that call or return it quickly. Failure to respond may mean missed coverage for you and your book.

Don't ask to see copy in advance

If the journalist tells you he is writing up the piece for next Thursday's edition, don't ask to see a copy in advance. Journalists don't like doing this as experience shows them that some people can't resist dabbling with the style or changing their minds about what they said.

Do not be aggressive or combative towards a journalist

Some journalists might be quite aggressive in the way

they question you. This does not necessarily mean they are hostile but trying to tease out a good story. If you get aggressive back you will only aggravate them and could end up with a negative story into the bargain. Stay focused and remain polite.

Always have ready a few well-rehearsed statements or key points about your book that you would like to make

This will help you in leading the interview rather than just responding to it.

Maintain a friendly relationship with journalists

If a journalist can rely on you to feed him good stories and provide information, you will increase your chances of winning more media coverage.

Don't hound a journalist to find out when your story is likely to appear

Journalists don't like this. Besides, if you do follow up the release you may not get the truth. It isn't that the journalist will deliberately lie to you (although some may), it is just that they are under pressure and may genuinely not know if they will use the story. And even if they have decided to use it, the editor may cut the story because of more pressing news items that have arisen during the day or the week.

If you get a bad review, ignore it; don't dash off a rude email or make an angry telephone call. You got a mention, didn't you – and as the saying goes – there's no such thing as bad publicity!

Which media should you target?

This depends on the type of book you have written. If you have defined your readers then you should have an idea of which newspapers and magazines they might read, or which television and radio programmes they like. Don't just think about book review programmes and book reviewers but think laterally. For example with my marine mysteries I targeted the national sailing media as well as my local media.

Different types of media

There are many different types of media. Here are some of them.

- national newspapers
- daily newspapers
- sunday newspapers
- local newspapers
- daily local newspapers
- weekly local newspapers
- bi-weekly local newspapers
- freesheets
- community newspapers
- specialist magazines
- professional and trade press
- consumer magazines
- local radio
- national radio

- local television
- national television including cable and satellite channels
- internet or new media

Researching the media list

Once you have defined your target reader you can begin to research your media list. There are various publications that can assist you with this. These can be found in the reference section of your library. Some are also available online.

I have listed a few of the publications that may help you. This list is by no means exhaustive.

- BRAD (British Rates & Data)
- *Willings Press Guide*
- *The Guardian Media Guide*

The Internet

Alternatively you can search on the Internet if you know the name of the publication or television/radio station you wish to target.

The Commercial Radio Company Association

www.crca.co.uk provides contact details of all the commercial radio stations.

Targeting the media

When planning to target magazines you need to be

aware that most if not all monthly publications work on features three, sometimes six months ahead of publication, so getting the timing right is critical.

Once you have identified the magazines you wish to target, you can telephone the publication and ask for a media pack and a feature list. (Or you can check this information out on their web site.) A list of magazine personnel is often displayed at the front of a publication giving telephone numbers and email addresses.

A feature list can help you plan for future news stories.

Obtain a copy of the publication and study it for content to make sure that your news story is suitable for the magazine and to enable you to tailor it, if necessary, to suit the publication's readers.

In newspapers, study the articles and features. Do you have a story about your book, or taken from the content of your book, that might make a good feature article? (See chapter 13.) You will find that in most newspapers the journalist's name and sometimes an email address are given at the end of the article.

Put the contact details onto a database, if possible, as it will be easier to update and manage. Journalists frequently change jobs and it is quite a task keeping track of them.

In summary

- building a positive media profile is one of the most effective ways you can promote your book

- the best way of getting media coverage is to send in a news release

- be aware of editorial style when submitting your news release to different types of media and tailor it accordingly

- you can engage a publicist to write your news releases but you will need to budget for this

- try to provide editors and journalists with stories they will want and which are suitable for them

- always try and be accessible to the media, don't ask to see copy in advance and do not be aggressive or combative towards a journalist

- have ready a few well-rehearsed statements or key points about your book

- don't hound a journalist to find out when your story is likely to appear

- if you get a bad review ignore it, don't dash off a rude email or make an angry phone call

- define your target reader and research your media list

- be aware that many monthly publications work on features in advance

- telephone the publication and ask for a media pack and a feature list to help you plan future news stories

- study a copy of the publication for content to make sure your news story is suitable

- put the journalist/editor contact details onto a database – it will be easier to update

10

News stories and angles

'Author launches new book' is not really a story – there are thousands of books launched every year.

'Local author launches new book' sent to a local newspaper is a stronger story because as you can see it is capitalising on **the local angle.**

'Local author overcomes tremendous odds to launch new book' is even more of a story capitalising on the **human interest angle**.

And that is what you need to do to get media coverage (particularly if you are not famous) – you need to **find the angle.**

Finding the angle can be extremely difficult for some people but with a bit of imagination it is possible.

Is your book about a topical subject? Does it go against all the evidence and is therefore controversial? Do you have something new to say? Is it the first of its kind?

Are *you* the angle for your news story? Have you overcome huge odds to produce this book? Would it make interesting reading? Have you led a fascinating life, rubbed shoulders with the rich and famous, danced with death?

Is your book somehow linked with a local or national charity and has their endorsement? Or perhaps it has celebrity endorsement.

Are you giving a talk to a local writers' or readers' group? Or perhaps speaking at a conference or running a writing workshop? All these are worthy of news releases.

Does the launch of the book coincide with any anniversaries? Is it an ideal book for:

- Valentine's Day
- Mother's Day
- Christmas
- Bonfire Night
- other anniversaries

Are you old or young? For example are you publishing your book at the age of 85 or 15?

Are you a male writing about a female subject or vice versa, for example: 'Female bricklayer reveals all on the building sites of Britain in her new book!'

> The secret to getting coverage is having the right story to tell in the right way to the right media.

If you are serious about getting media coverage for your book and yourself then you need to start listening to, and reading about, what makes the news. If you hear or read something that touches your subject matter then why not write a news release on it and send it to the journalist, perhaps giving the opposing view. At least write a letter to the editor.

Writing the news release

There is a style and structure to writing the news release and by following it you will increase your chances of gaining media coverage.

> When constructing a news release you need to think of a triangle or pyramid.

The whole story, including the angle, is contained in the first paragraph and then the story is fleshed out in subsequent paragraphs. If you study newspapers you will see this style in evidence.

But first a couple of don'ts:

Don't use cliché's and hyperbole – the 'best novel of the year' type thing – 'the new J.K. Rowling' etc.

Don't use excessive adjectives and super-latives; this is a concise, informative news release, telling the journalist about your book, you and/or your news story. Leave the rest to the journalist.

Constructing the news release

Headline – an idea of what the story is about

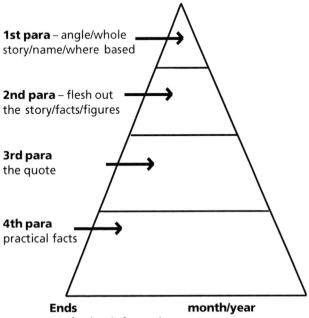

1st para – angle/whole story/name/where based

2nd para – flesh out the story/facts/figures

3rd para the quote

4th para practical facts

Ends   **month/year**
For further information contact:
name,   location, telephone,
email address.

The news release – step by step

Let's start at the top of our triangle.

The headline

This must encapsulate the story. The headline is there to catch the journalist's eye and tell him what the story is about. Your headline will rarely be used by the newspaper or magazine. The journalist, editor or sub-editor will put their own title to the story which best fits the style of their publication. Your headline might only be used if you are writing an article to commission or you have paid to see the article printed. In the latter case we are not talking about editorial but advertising or advertorial. You may want to come back to writing your headline after you have read the following sections and written your news release.

Example of a headline

New book aims to help managers boost face-to-face communication skills

This headline tells the journalist what the news release is about. It also tells the journalist that it is aimed at the business market.

The first paragraph

This is the key to the release. It must contain the whole story, the angle, who you are and where you are based. Can you tell your whole story in one short paragraph?

This is for two reasons: the journalist can save time by reading the first paragraph and make a quick decision whether or not the news story is of interest to him, and when a news release is edited by the journalist it is often from the bottom upwards which means that if you are squeezed out by space issues then at least you stand a chance of getting your first paragraph in the newspaper or magazine if nothing else.

Here is an example of a first paragraph following on from our headline.

Example of a first paragraph

A new book, *The Easy Step by Step Guide to Communicating with More Confidence*, by Pauline Rowson, aims to help managers and others in the workplace boost their face-to-face communication skills at a time when email and text is fast replacing the spoken word.

The above paragraph contains the essence of the story. It tells the journalist the name of the book, what it is about and the angle i.e. face-to-face communication skills are being lost.

I could adapt this news release for local media for example:

A new book, *The Easy Step by Step Guide to Communicating with More Confidence*, by Hampshire based author Pauline Rowson, aims to help managers and others in the workplace boost their face-to-face communication skills at a time when email and text is fast replacing the spoken word.

The second paragraph

This goes on to give the details already summarized in paragraph one. You may only need one paragraph of explanation; otherwise two will probably be sufficient. Here I have used two.

Here is an example following through our news story.

Mrs Rowson claims that many managers are finding it increasingly difficult to handle the sensitive interview, give presentations and tackle difficult staff confidently, preferring to hide behind their computers and email when criticizing and giving instructions.

Communicating with More Confidence looks at how to improve communication skills through boosting self-confidence, understanding and reading body language and learning how to begin, structure and close conversations. It also examines communicating at social and business events, how to conduct interviews and how to relate to and manage the different personalities.

The third or fourth paragraph

This is usually the quote.

Pauline Rowson says, 'There are many young people starting working life not knowing how to talk to their colleagues let alone customers and bosses and many would rather use email than pick up a telephone. People lack the confidence to tackle difficult situations face-to-face, seeking to chastize and even dismiss people by email. When you look at almost any struggling company or organisation it is often poor communication that is at the heart of the problem.'

The final paragraph

If the release is about a new publication or event it can give a contact name and telephone number.

For example:

*Communi*cating with More Confidence *costs £9.99 and is available from UK bookshops or direct from the publisher Rowmark on 023 9246 1931.*

After this you should write **ENDS** and the date, then **'for further information contact'** and give contact details for the journalist or editor.

Here is the complete news release.

News Release.......News Release............

New book aims to help managers boost face-to-face communication skills

A new book, *The Easy Step by Step Guide to Communicating with More Confidence*, by Pauline Rowson, aims to help managers and others in the workplace boost their face-to-face communication skills at a time when email and text is fast replacing the spoken word.

Mrs. Rowson claims that many managers are finding it increasingly difficult to handle the sensitive interview, give presentations and tackle difficult staff confidently, preferring to hide behind their computers and email when criticizing and giving instructions.

Communicating with More Confidence looks at how to improve communication skills through boosting self confidence, understanding and reading body language and learning how to begin, structure and close conversations. It also examines communicating at social and business events; how to conduct interviews and how to relate to and manage the different personalities.

Pauline Rowson says, 'There are many young people starting working life not knowing how to talk to their colleagues let alone customers and bosses and many would rather use email than pick up a telephone. People lack the confidence to tackle difficult situations face-to-face seeking to chastize and even dismiss people by email. When you look at almost any struggling company or organisation it is often poor communication that is at the heart of the problem.'

Communicating with More Confidence costs £9.99 and is available from UK bookshops or direct from the publisher Rowmark on 023 9246 1931.

Ends   Date

For further information and a review copy contact:

Pauline Rowson

023 9246 1931

email: pauline@rowmark.co.uk

www.rowmark.co.uk

Notes to the Editors

About the author

Pauline Rowson lives in the UK and has worked in marketing and PR for over twenty years. She is a writer and professional conference speaker who has helped countless individuals and businesses improve their communication skills. Her books include The Easy Step by Step Guides to *Successful Selling, Telemarketing, Cold Calling & Appointment Making, Marketing, Building a Positive*

Media Profile, and *Being Positive and Staying Positive*.

Notes to the editor provide a little more information about the author, which the journalist can include if he or she wishes.

News release layout guide

Before you send your release to the media you should also note the following guidance on layout and style.

- print **news release** across the top of the paper (this tells the journalist that it is information that can be printed)

- type neatly with one-and-a-half line spacing and wide margins

- use only one side of paper

- don't underline anything

This implies that you are trying to tell the journalist what is important. They don't need you to tell them how to do their job. Besides, what is important to you may not be so important to the journalist.

- if you go onto a second page, put 'more follows ....' at the bottom of the first page

- don't split a sentence or a paragraph between one page and the next

- staple the pages together if you are posting the release

- avoid jargon, be as factual as possible

- get someone to proofread it for mistakes before it goes out

- send by first class post, email or fax, and wherever

possible address to the journalist by name

Embargoes

An embargo in its strictest sense, as taken from the Oxford Dictionary, means an order forbidding foreign ships to enter or leave the country's ports, or suspension of commerce. In the media sense it means an order forbidding the media to use the release until the sender gives permission.

You may wish to tell the journalist that your book is being released on a certain date but do not want them to print the story before then so that people who read the article are immediately able to purchase the book.

The media will generally honour an embargo and it is certainly useful for them from a planning point of view to have information about the story or book before its official release.

It is usually common practice to write at the top of your release **'Embargo – Not to be used before midday on (the date)'**.

Do you need a photograph?

You can send a photograph with the news release to the journalist but make sure the photograph is of high quality. Wherever possible you should enlist the services of a professional photographer. It will cost you but it could be worth it.

Brief the photographer thoroughly beforehand, as she or he may need to bring along additional equipment or film, and do ensure you are available when they arrive or you could be charged for waiting time.

Magazines and newspapers now accept, and indeed prefer, digital images so you should ensure that your photographer can shoot digitally and then email you the photographs as jpg files. If the technology is beyond you, don't worry; as long as you have a good colour photograph you can always send that to the newspaper or magazine. If you are posting your news release, attach your colour photograph to the release and write on the back who is in the picture.

Doing it yourself

You may wish to take your own photographs rather than use a professional photographer. By all means do so, but you need to ensure that you take the right type of shots.

Please bear in mind that the shots need to be close-up. Most amateurs tend to go for the long shot – you know, someone sitting behind a table or desk, and all you can see is acres of table and a tiny person at the end. This will never get into print. Most magazines and newspapers crop shots and they can't do this if there is a mass of scenery.

Make a study of the photographs in the newspapers and magazines to see what style they like and try and emulate it.

Press photographers

Some people think that the newspaper is obliged to send a photographer if they ask them to, but this is not the case.

Newspaper photographers have many calls upon their time and they could be on an assignment that the editor views as far more important than yours. For example, a fire in a tower block is going to be more newsworthy than your book launch, even if the local MP is attending!

Newspapers and magazines no longer have lots of staff photographers; in fact, some have none at all and the reporter is expected to take his own photographs whilst interviewing the client. This often happens on the local/regional newspapers.

If, however, the magazine or newspaper is sufficiently interested to send along its photographer then please be understanding about their other assignments; if they are late they may have been called to another story breaking and been delayed. The media are responding to as well as making the news.

Be aware that if a press photographer is coming to take your photograph, they will advise you on the shots they require – so a couple of words of caution here.

Do not be bullied or cajoled into shots that you would not like to see in print.

Don't get into any pose that makes you uncomfortable.

I was once asked to pose lying down on my sofa! Needless to say I refused.

In summary

- start to develop a journalistic eye and a journalistic mind

- the secret to getting coverage is having the right story to tell in the right way to the right media

- always look for the angle

- the headline of your news release must encapsulate the story

- the whole story – including the angle – should be contained in the first paragraph and then the story is fleshed out in subsequent paragraphs

- type neatly with generous line spacing and wide margins and use only one side of paper

- don't underline anything and if you go on to a second page, put 'more follows ....' at the bottom of the first page

- don't split a sentence or a paragraph between one page and the next

- photographs should be colour and good quality

- you can send photographs to the media as a jpg file attached to your email message but ensure they are high resolution.

11
The radio interview

When asked if you would like to contribute to a radio or television programme, you could experience all of the following reactions: delight, horror, excitement, dread and sheer blind panic – and all in a matter of seconds. Many people are flattered to be asked and automatically agree without really knowing what they are agreeing to. In this chapter I have provided you with a list of questions that you should ask before blindly accepting the opportunity to be in the limelight. Nevertheless it is a very good opportunity to promote your book

Questions to ask:

1   What made you contact me?
    (Unless they have already told you that it is in response to a news release you sent them or a press item they have seen in the local newspaper.)

2   What kind of programme is it?

When does it go out? Who listens to/watches it?

3 Is it live or recorded and will I be interviewed live or recorded?

4 How long will the interview/session last?

5 Is anyone else being interviewed or contributing to the programme?

6 Is there audience participation? Are there any phone-ins that I am expected to respond to, or is it a straight interview?

7 Where will the interview take place?
   The interview could take place in a number of locations. It may be:

- on a phone-in from your office or home – a 'down the line' interview

- in the radio or television studio

- on location

- in the radio or television car

- in a remote studio.

Once you have satisfied yourself on the above points and have decided that you are happy to give the interview, you will need to prepare for it.

First, don't assume the interviewer will have read your book; he or she most probably hasn't.

If you are invited on to the show don't go into overkill on plugging the book, use the opportunity to show that you are an interesting person with a good story to tell. Keep it casual, be entertaining and co-operative.

Think about the image of the book that you want the listeners (or viewers if a television interview) to go away with. This will help them to remember the book rather than you and hopefully they will then go into their library to borrow it or into a bookshop to buy it.

The 'down the line interview'

This is when the interview is conducted with a radio interviewer over the telephone. You are in your own surroundings, so hopefully you are more relaxed.

On the radio, as on the telephone, your voice needs to convey a great deal about you. People will judge you on how you sound. So give your voice some training.

Record yourself into a Dictaphone or on quality audio equipment and play it back. How does your voice sound?

Now, try reading an excerpt from your book or some poetry. Put expression into your voice and get used to the nuances of it. What do you like or dislike about your voice? What do you need to do to make it sound more lively and interesting?

Listen to radio programmes – what makes you listen to some people and turn others off?

Don't worry if you have a regional accent. Provided people can understand you, accents bring warmth and personality to your voice.

The sound bite

The radio and television interview is often short, sometimes no longer than three minutes. Everyone is familiar with the term 'sound bites' these days, so practice yours or at least talk into a dictaphone for three minutes, and listen to how long it sounds. Can you sum up what your book is about, why you wrote it and any other major point you wish to get across in three minutes? Many people get too verbose in interviews and if it is recorded they will edit you – sometimes completely.

The radio studio

You may be asked to go into the studio for your interview. Some people find this easier to deal with than the 'down the line' interview, as they feel they are at least in the appropriate surroundings and there are experts on hand to help if anything goes wrong.

You will be asked to arrive about ten minutes before your interview is due to take place. This can seem daunting to some people, who would prefer to be at the studio about half an hour before to prepare themselves.

The time-frame on radio and television takes some getting used to. Presenters develop an immaculate sense of timing in seconds and whilst you are hopping up and down, wondering if they will ever make the deadline, they are still wandering around getting themselves a coffee or reading the newspaper seconds before they go on air. Trust them – they are the professionals.

However, having said that, it is best that you arrive at the studio with some time to spare. You will need to allow for the usual: traffic delays, the need to visit the toilet, the need to tidy yourself – even if you are only appearing on radio – and the need to glance through your notes and still your pounding heart.

It is also a good idea to listen to the radio programme on which you are about to feature before arriving at the studio. Perhaps you can have it playing in your car and then you can get a feel for the programme and how the presenter is advertising you. Is the programme friendly and chatty or has it a businesslike style? Always aim to be friendly and professional in your approach.

You have already asked whether or not the interview is live. If it is live, you are safe to say good morning or good evening in your opening remark. If the programme is recorded, you may like to check what time of day it will be broadcast, or play on the safe side and simply say 'Hello' when the presenter introduces you.

The radio studio is usually dark and invariably small. You will usually be seated across a console from the radio presenter and there will be a microphone in front of you or suspended from the ceiling. You may be asked to wear earphones and the technicians will test the volume (level) of your voice before going on air.

Always ask the presenter what his or her first question is going to be. They usually stick to this, unless they want to be awkward, or your book is controversial. With radio, of course, you can have your notes in front of you, but beware of looking down at them all the time or moving your head away from the microphone.

Remember the audience wants to listen to you and understand what you are saying; they want to be informed and entertained.

The remote studio

Going into a remote studio is a daunting experience

for many people. There is often no one in the studio or perhaps one journalist who is working on another story and leaves you to it.

In the immortal words of Corporal Jones in the comedy series, *Dad's Army* 'Don't Panic'.

Follow the instructions (usually written up and stuck to the desk or wall) which asks you to dial into the main studio. Once you have done this a technician will talk you through what you have to do. He or she will ask you to put on the earphones and then test the level of your voice. Then the presenter will speak to you and will run through the basic idea of the interview and the sort of things he wishes to discuss.

Points to remember for good radio interviewing

Here are some tips to help you conduct a good radio interview.

- aim for a friendly conversational style – be as natural as you can
- know your audience and the purpose of the interview
- for local radio, keep it as local as you can

Tape an interview

Radio stations are usually looking for items to use as fillers on certain programmes. You could use the facilities of a studio and an experienced freelance producer to produce a short tape in the form of an interview that can then be circulated to radio stations.

You can find details of commercial radio stations on www.crca.co.uk or contact the Commercial Radio Associations 020 7306 2603.

Alternatively you could use the services of Meet the Author www.meettheauthor.co.uk. Launched in 2004 the web site features Book Bites from over 500 authors. Book Bites are short video clips in which the author talks about his or her book. Book Bites are also featured on special displays in bookshops and have links to Amazon. Perhaps you could use this to circulate to radio and television producers?

In summary

- the 'down the line' interview is conducted over the telephone
- your body language and posture will affect how your voice sounds
- the radio and television interview is often short; practice your sound bites
- ask the presenter what his or her first question is going to be
- always aim to be friendly and professional in your approach

12

The television interview

Again, as with the radio interview, the researcher or the producer will contact you to ask if you would like to participate in the programme. Before succumbing to the flattery of being asked and agreeing eagerly, calm yourself and go through your checklist of questions.

1 Why are you asking me?

2 What kind of programme is it?

3 Is it live or pre-recorded?

4 Who will be interviewing me?

5 What is the slant or the angle of the interview/programme?

6 Am I being interviewed or is it a discussion? If it's a discussion, who else is participating?

7 When is it being transmitted?

8 Where will the interview be held?

9 How long is my contribution likely to be?

Remember you can always say no – though few people do because they are so flattered at being asked. And again this could be a great opportunity for you to promote your book.

There are different types of television interviewing. These include:

- live interviews either in the television studio or on location
- pre-recorded interviews
- 'as for live' interviews.

'As for live' interviews

'As for live' are interviews where the recording is not stopped unless something goes disastrously wrong and the interview will be timed by the interviewer to run for the allotted length of time. Programmes like *Question Time* are conducted in this way.

Pre-recorded interviews

With pre-recorded interviews, the presenter can take longer with you, the questions stretch on and you begin to relax and let your guard down – which means the edited version may only show those shots towards the end of the interview where you are being rather more verbose than you should!

The television studio

When asked to attend an interview in a television studio, try to allow enough time to reach the studio without being too rushed. Find the toilet and try to settle yourself. Don't give yourself too much time or your nervous tension can mount.

Don't be tempted to have a stiff drink before appearing, or drink tea or coffee. Stick to water.

Remember that nothing is ever 'off the record', so don't reveal anything you don't want to be used to anyone in the studio – they may feed this information to the interviewer, who could then use it in the programme to throw you off your stride.

When you meet your interviewer, try and ask him or her what the first question is to be. I say try, because that may be difficult. You may not have time to see him before the interview and you will also have other people wiring you up with a microphone and positioning you in the chair etc.

Television studios are bright and hot and the glare of the lights takes some getting used to. The television studio is also a lot smaller than many people imagine. If you get the chance to visit one before your interview, take it. Being familiar with your surroundings will help you when the time comes to be interviewed.

If the studio hasn't been laid out it looks very much like an empty room except for some cables lying around. When dressed for the set, seating is usually arranged around the 'stage' in ranks – a bit like a theatre – and there are usually two or three cameras on moveable pedestals.

The director will, from his control room, be able to select from a range of shots of those taking part in the programme. Although a red light will appear on the camera currently being used, do not attempt to try and follow this red light – it will only confuse you. But do remember that even when you believe you are off camera to act as if you are still on camera. You don't want to be caught unawares.

> **Treat every camera as if it is rolling and on you.**

In addition, treat every microphone as if it is live. Try not to fiddle with your tie or scarf as the microphone will be positioned there and will crackle dreadfully. All microphones amplify the normal voice so there is no need to shout, or use a special voice like you see some comics doing deliberately on television shows and dramas. Speak as you would in normal conversation and let the technicians do the rest.

The interviewer normally has a monitor in front of him. Do not look at that, or the cameras, but concentrate your attention on, and direct your conversation to, the interviewer. If asked a question by someone in the audience (if it is that type of programme), look at the questioner when you answer him, as you would in real life.

If you are running out of things to say, or feel you are drying up, or don't know the answer to the question, then if you are looking at the interviewer he will know this by the look in your eyes (probably sheer terror!) and will help you out.

Above all, try to relax and be natural – which seems an impossibility given all I have said!

On location

When the media turn up on your doorstep, they can be completely overwhelming, even if it is only the reporter and the cameraman. So here is some advice for you when dealing with the television crew:

Whether the interview is in the studio or in your own home always treat the microphone as if it is live and the camera as if it is running.

Never say or do anything that you wouldn't like to see appear on your television screen.

If you are being interviewed on location, then check the backdrop against which you will be filmed. We have all seen out-takes where what is going on behind the interview is more interesting than the actual interview.

In many instances, the media will come to your home. Make sure the environment is giving out the right impression.

What to wear on television

- avoid houndstooth-type checks, boldly striped jackets and suits, shirts and ties
- avoid very white blouses and shirts: they cause glare
- avoid anything too tight and restricting and make sure your jacket doesn't gape when you sit

- don't flash the flesh – make sure your socks are long enough to meet your trousers and are the same colour as your trousers and shoes.

- don't wear flashy jewellery that glints and women should not wear heavy bracelets or dangling earrings that distract attention

- women should watch the length of their skirt – not so short that it rides up and shows more flesh than it should, not too tight or with a long split in it that flashes the thigh

- women should go for unfussy styles. Cleavage should be concealed at all times unless your book is about sex or that is the angle you wish to promote! Always wear plain tights, not patterned, and check they are ladder-free.

- check your shoulders for dandruff and make sure your hair is groomed and tidy

- a dusting of translucent powder for both men and women can help prevent that shiny look. The days when make-up artists at studios were ever at the ready are gone, so you may have to bring your own

- ensure your spectacles suit the shape of your face and do not swamp it. Never wear tinted glasses or lenses that darken in the light, as they will give you a shifty look.

And watch those mannerisms

Do not:

- clench and unclench hands
- fiddle with objects

- keep buttoning and unbuttoning your jacket

- drum your fingers on the table top

- jiggle your legs.

Do

- have water to hand; your mouth will feel dry – it's the nerves

- avoid tea, coffee and alcohol; these are dehydrating and alcohol can have disastrous consequences.

- try to be natural and allow your real self to shine through on television and radio, even though this can be difficult because of nerves.

In summary

- treat every microphone as if it is live and the camera as if it is running

- never say or do anything that you wouldn't like to see appear on your television screen

- arrive early at the studio and settle yourself down as much as possible

- ask yourself, 'What two or three key things about me/my book do I want the viewer to remember?'

- remember that nothing is ever 'off the record', so don't reveal anything you don't want to be used to anyone in the studio

- when you meet your interviewer, try and ask them what their first question is to be

- all microphones amplify the normal voice, so there is no need to shout or use a special voice; speak as you would in normal conversation

- try to relax and be natural

- if you are being interviewed on location, check the backdrop against which you will be filmed.

13
Articles and talks

Writing articles

Writing articles and getting them into magazines and newspapers is a good way of raising your profile and that of your book/s. There are plenty of books on the market covering this subject one of which is *The Easy Step by Step Guide to Writing Newsletters and Articles,* so in this chapter I will give only a brief overview of article writing and explain how to get an article commissioned.

Getting a commission

First know what topic or topics you wish to write about, which should be easy for you as they may be based on your book/s.

Next you will need to research your media, what sort of magazines and newspapers would be interested in this subject matter?

Again, I would urge you to send for a media pack and to study the editorial content of the publication for which you wish to write. What sort of articles do they carry? What is their style?

Having done this, what do you think you can write about that readers would be interested in? Come up with an idea, or a topic, or even a few ideas.

After this you can approach the editor, usually in writing or by email, to see if he/she is interested. In your letter or email you will need to:

- give an outline of your idea
- say why you think the readers will be interested in what you have to say
- outline the treatment of the idea/topic
- say what makes it different
- explain the expertise you have to bring to the article

In fact, give the editor reasons why he should commission you to write this article.

If the editor is interested in commissioning this article, then you can ask:

1 How many words would they like?

2 When will the article appear?

3 When does the editor require the article by?

4 Is any special approach or treatment required?

5 Are illustrations or photographs required?

Other ways of being commissioned

You may be asked to write an article following the submission of a news release. Or you may have sent a letter to the editor and then been contacted to write an article on the subject.

(Don't forget that letters to the editor are another good way of getting your name and/or book into print.)

Getting paid

Not all magazines or newspapers will pay you for writing articles. If your objective is to gain experience and increase your personal profile and that of your book, then you may be willing to write the article for free in exchange for a mention of your book at the end of the article.

If a magazine or newspaper does pay, then they will give you some idea of their rates.

Giving talks

Giving talks to groups of people is an excellent way to promote your book. But speaking in public can and does terrify many people. In order to overcome this fear there is much you can do in advance. For more information on this see *The Easy Step by Step Guide to Giving Confident Presentations* and *The Easy Step by Step Guide to Communicating with more Confidence*.

Planning and preparation are critical factors in giving a successful talk. Telling yourself that it isn't a matter of life or death, no one expects you to be orator of the year, is also an important factor.

Research local organisations and groups and identify those who might be interested in hearing you speak about your book e.g. Rotary clubs, Women's Institutes, local writers groups, other interest groups etc.

Write to them sending a promotional leaflet on your book offering to give a talk to their members/group.

If a date is fixed then send a news release to the target media giving information about the talk (if the organisers are happy with this) and arrange for someone to take a photograph at the event which you could send out after the event with another news release.

When speaking, be conscious of the audience and what they might want to hear; communicate your own enthusiasm and belief in your book. Talk about the content of the book but don't go on and on about it – you want to give them enough information to whet their appetite so that they buy a copy. Find something funny, different or unusual to reveal, perhaps some of the frustrations or the extraordinary facts unearthed during the research.

Have some books with you so that people can buy a copy, give out leaflets for those who don't buy then but might later call in at their bookshop or contact you for a copy.

In summary

- writing articles and getting them into magazines

and newspapers is a good way of raising your profile and that of your book/s.

- articles are generally written to commission
- every magazine and newspaper has its own editorial policy and style so get to know it
- research your media, send for a media pack and study the editorial style and content
- approach the editor, usually in writing or by email, to see if he is interested in your ideas
- research local organisations and groups and identify those who might be interested in hearing you speak about your book
- write to them sending a promotional leaflet on your book and offering to give a talk
- communicate your own enthusiasm and belief in your book
- talk about the content of the book but don't go on and on about it, just whet their appetite so that they buy a copy
- find something funny, different or unusual to reveal
- have books with you so that people can buy a copy.

14

The launch party

Launch parties used to be the standard way for publishers to launch a new book but with the pressure on budgets only the famous and potentially **big** titles and authors now get the launch party. If you are published by a publishing house and are not one of their **big** titles/author then you may need to organize your own launch party on a local level and some publishers will be happy to pay towards the cost of this. If you are self-publishing then you need to decide if a launch party would be a good use of your money and an effective way to promote your book.

Local media could very well be attracted to a local launch particularly if your book is newsworthy or topical, or has some interesting local flavour. Conducting a book launch for one of my Easy Step by Step Guides would not be very interesting or exciting. I can achieve the same amount of coverage in the local media by simply issuing a news release. But having a book launch for one of my marine mysteries is different. Why? Because these books have a wider readership, I can tie in with a local bookshop, I can conduct the launch at a local marina or yacht club, and I can invite friends, family, contacts, the media – both local and the national sailing fraternity. It will however cost me. So unless I simply wish to have a party I need to justify if the expense will be worth it.

> **The key aims are for you to raise the profile of your book and sell as many signed copies at the event as possible.**

Invitees

Who you are looking to attract?

- journalists, both from your target media and freelancers but don't expect them to attend, even if they have promised to, as they are notoriously bad at showing up

- librarians and other key people from organisations in your area

- local booksellers

- family and friends, and encourage them to circulate to ensure no one is on his or her own

- a photographer to capture the event and take some shots for you to send to journalists who didn't attend, along with a press release after the event.

The newspaper and magazine journalists could arrive with their own photographers and if so, great! Build in some time for photographs to be taken and journalists to ask you questions.

What day and time should the launch be held?

This depends on your type of book and the typical reader. A weekday evening is probably best as people may be working during the day. A weekend may be more suitable if your book is a children's book. Allow for a maximum of two hours giving your guests time to mill around, eat, drink and talk to other people as well as to you about your book.

Check out conflicting events

You do not want a book launch to conflict with the launch of major national exhibition, or an important anniversary that the journalists will be covering, unless of course your book launch is arranged around the exhibition.

Choose your venue

Try and choose an unusual venue, which may encourage more journalists to attend and which could be linked to your book. This will add a distinctive flavour to your news story.

Alternatively your local library or bookshop may be happy to host the event, or the local Arts Centre. Or perhaps you are a member of a club or society whose room you could hire.

Pay attention to detail

Is there power for electrical equipment and a quiet area for interviews if required? Is there ample parking

– very important? Or is the venue easily accessible by local transport? Is the food and drink adequate? Do you hire a catering company or will the venue do it? Do you want waiters and waitresses circulating or is it a buffet?

Post someone on the door to welcome people and answer queries – you can't be everywhere. Also brief them to keep an eye open for any journalists and to give you the nod if they arrive.

The invitation

Is your book launch open to members of the public or by invitation only? If members of the public can attend then make sure you send a press release to the media beforehand informing them of this.

If by invitation then send it out well in advance as people's diaries do get booked up. Aim for at least a month before the event, six weeks if you can. If inviting journalists then send the invite out with enough information to whet the editor or journalist's appetite.

Enclose a map giving directions to the venue and parking and include an RSVP slip or phone number.

The format

Make sure that everyone has a drink on arrival and once you believe everyone has arrived, or you have allowed a reasonable time, get someone else to introduce you to the audience; perhaps the bookshop owner or librarian, or a key person who can then hand over to you, the author. Thank your host, say a little bit about the book, be entertaining and don't talk for too long. Ten minutes should be sufficient, any longer than this and people will start to get bored.

The press pack

Have copies of a prepared news release and promotional flyers readily available.

Ensure there are enough copies of your book to hand.

After the launch

Write to all those who showed up and thank them.

Write to journalists (or email them) to thank them for coming or for the subsequent media coverage, and see if you can use the opportunity to discuss any further features but don't pester them. To those who didn't show, send the news release and photograph.

In summary

- local media may be attracted to a launch particularly if your book is newsworthy, or topical, or has some interesting local flavour

- the key aims are for you to raise the profile of your book and sell as many signed copies at the event as possible

- build in some time for photographs to be taken and journalists to ask you questions

- a weekday evening is probably the best time to hold the launch. A weekend may be more suitable if your book is a children's book

- allow for a maximum of two hours giving your guests time to mill around, eat, drink and talk to other people as well as to you about your book

- check out conflicting events

- try and choose an unusual venue which may encourage more journalists to attend

- have copies of a prepared news release and flyers readily available

- ensure there are enough copies of your book to hand

- after the launch write to all those who showed up and thank them

- to those who didn't show, send the news release and photograph.

And finally …

Before publication of your book draw up a programme of marketing activity simply stating what you need to do and when and if possible how much it is going to cost you so that you can budget more effectively.

Give yourself enough time before publishing your book to plan for how you are going to launch it and promote it.

Obtain costs to print and produce your book and to produce marketing material – add this to your budget.

If you are trying to find a publisher or agent for your book, ensure that your work is of the highest standard possible and comply with their submission requests.

Listen to advice, take criticism on the chin, improve and hone your skill, and above all **never give up.**

Happy writing!

Useful organizations and addresses

Writing

The Society of Authors
84 Drayton Gardens
London SW10 9SB
Tel: 020 7373 6642
Fax: 020 7373 5768
info@societyofauthors.org
www.societyofauthors.org

The Writers Guild of Great
Britain
15 Britannia Street
London WC1X 9JN
Tel: 020 7833 0777
Fax: 020 7833 4777
admin@writersguild.org.uk
www.writersguild.org.uk

Booktrust
45 East Hill
London SW18 2QZ
Tel: 020 8516 2977
Fax: 020 8516 2978
www.booktrust.org.uk

(Information sheets on Grants, Awards and Bursuries)

Writers News
1st Floor Victoria House
143–145 The Headrow
Leeds LS1 5RL
Subscriptions: 01778 392 482
Editorial: 0113 200 2913
www.writersnews.co.uk

Writing Magazine
Subscriptions: 01778 392 482
Editorial: 0113 200 2913
www.writingmagazine.co.uk

Authors Licensing & Collecting
Society Ltd.
Marlborough Court
14–18 Holborn
London EC1N 2LE
Tel: 020 7395 0600
Fax: 020 7395 0660
E mail: alcs@alcs.co.uk
www.alcs.co.uk

Agents

Association of Authors'
Agents
Drury House
34–43 Russell Street
London WC2B 5HA
Tel: 020 7344 1000
Fax: 020 7836 9541
E mail: aaa@pfd.co.uk
www.agentsassoc.co.uk

The book trade

Publishing News
7 John Street
London WC1N 2ES
Tel: 0870 870 2345
Fax:0870 870 0385
Editorial fax: 0207 404 7698
mailbox@publishingnews.co.uk
www.publishingnews co.uk

The Bookseller
Endeavour House
5th Floor
189 Shaftesbury Avenue
London WC2H 8TJ
Tel: 01795 414953
www.theBookseller.com

British Printing Industries
Federation
Farringdon Point
29-35 Farringdon Road
London EC1M 3JF
Tel: 0870 240 4085
Fax: 020 7405 7784
info@bpif.org.uk
www.britishprint.com

Independent Publishers Guild
PO Box 93
Royston
Hertfordshire SG8 5GH
Tel: 01763 247014
Fax: 01763 246293
info@ipg.uk.com
www.ipg.uk.com

The Publishers Association
29B Montague Street
London WC1B 5BW
Tel: 020 7691 9191
Fax: 020 7691 9199
mail@publishers.org.uk
www.publishers.org.uk

The Booksellers Association
Limited
272 Vauxhall Bridge Road
London SW1V 1BA
Tel: 020 7802 0802

*Cassells Directory of
Publishing*: an annual
publication listing the majority
of UK publishers, their areas
of specialism and their
personnel. Published in
conjunction with the
Publishers Association.

*Guide to Export for UK Book
Publishers*
UK Trade & Investment
www.uktradeinvest.gov.uk
www.publishers.org.uk

Editorial

Society for Editors and
Proofreaders

Riverbank House
1 Putney Bridge Approach
London SW6 3JD
Tel: 020 7736 3278
Fax: 020 7736 3318
administration@sfep.org.uk
www.sfep.org.uk

Meet the Author
www.meettheauthor.co.uk

Publicity

Publishers Publicity Circle
www.publisherspublicity
circle.co.uk

Self-publishing

ISBN Agency
3rd Floor
Midas House
62 Goldsworth Road
Woking Surrey
GU21 6LQ
0870 777 8712
Fax: 0870 777 8714
E mail:
isbn@nielsenbookdata.co.uk
www.whitaker.co.uk/isbn.htm

Nielsen BookData
3rd Floor
Midas House
62 Goldsworth Road
Woking
Surrey GU21 6LQ
Tel: 0870 7778710
Fax: 0870 777 8711
E mail:
sales@nielsenbookdata.co.uk

Bowker UK Limited
3rd Floor Farringdon House,
Wood Street,
East Grinstead
West Sussex RH 19 1UZ
Tel: 01342 310463
Fax: 01342 310465

Publisher Liaison
BDS Limited
Annandale House
The Crichton
Bankend Road
Dumfries DG1 4TA
Tel: 01387 702251
Fax: 01387 702259
E mail: info@bibdsl.co.uk

Public Lending Right
Richard House
Sorbonne Close
Stockton On Tees
TS17 6DA
Tel: +44 (0) 1642 604699
Fax: +44 (0) 1642 615641

ALCS Limited
Marlborough Court
14–18 Holborn
London EC1N 2LE
Tel: 020 7395 0600
Fax: 020 7395 0660
E mail: alcs@alcs.co.uk
www.alcs.co.uk

Publishers Licensing Society
Limited
37–41 Gower Street
London WC1E 6HH
Telephone: 020 7299 7730
Fax: 020 7299 7780
E mail: pls@pls.org.uk
www.pls.org.uk

Help in producing your book

The Hilary Johnson Authors'
Advisory Service
1 Beechwood Court
Syderstone Norfolk PE31 8TR
Tel: 01485 578594
www.hilaryjohnson.com

Frances Hackeson
Freelance Publishing Services
38 Sandringham Drive
Brinscall, Chorley, Lancs. PR6
8SU
Tel: 01254 830059
www.hackeson.demon.co.uk
*editing, typesetting, book
interior and jacket/cover
design, advice and assistance
to self-publishers*

RPM Print and Design Ltd.
2-3 Spur Road
Quarry Lane Industrial Estate
Chichester West Sussex. PO19
8 PR
Tel: 01243 787077
Fax: 01243 780012
www.rpm-repro.co.uk
*Specialist printer for self-
publishers and publishers*

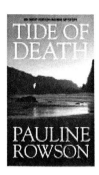

It is DI Andy Horton's second day back in Portsmouth CID after being suspended for eight months. Whilst out running in the early morning he stumbles over the naked battered body of a man on the beach. PC Evans has been stabbed the night before, the DCI is up before a promotion board and Sergeant Cantelli is having trouble with his fifteen-year-old daughter. But Horton's mind is on other things not least of which is trying to prove his innocence after being accused of raping Lucy Richardson.

Beset by personal problems and aided by Cantelli, Horton sets out to find a killer in the south coast town who will stop at nothing to cover his tracks. As he gets closer to the truth, and his personal investigations start to uncover dark secrets that someone would rather not have exposed, he risks not only his career but also his life.

ISBN:0955098203
Price: £6.99
Paperback

To order call 023 9246 1931
e mail enquiries@rowmark.co.uk
or visit our web site www.rowmark.co.uk

Fathom

Fathoming out another Marine Mystery!

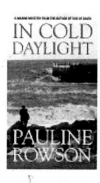

IN COLD DAYLIGHT

PAULINE ROWSON

Fire fighter Jack Bartholomew dies whilst trying to put out a fire in a derelict building. Was it an accident or arson? Marine artist Adam Greene doesn't know, only that he has lost his closest friend. He attends the funeral ready to mourn his friend only to find that another funeral intrudes upon his thoughts and one he's tried very hard to forget for the last fifteen years. But before he has time to digest this, or discover the identity of the stranger stalking him, Jack's house is ransacked.

Unaware of the risks he is running, Adam soon finds himself caught up in a mysterious and dangerous web of deceit. By exposing a secret that has lain dormant for years Adam is forced to face his own dark secrets and as the facts reveal themselves the prospects for his survival look bleak. But Adam knows there is no turning back, he has to get to the truth no matter what the cost, even if it is his life.

ISBN:0955098211
Price: £6.99
Paperback

To order call 023 9246 1931
e mail enquiries@rowmark.co.uk
or visit our web site www.rowmark.co.uk

Fathom

Fathoming out another Marine Mystery!